BIBLICAL EXEGESIS AND CHURCH DOCTRINE

Reflections on the interplay between the biblical criticism employed by almost all Roman Catholic scholars and the doctrinal proclamations of the Catholic Church. An attempt is made to explain why liberals and ultraconservatives alike misinterpret the effects of biblical criticism on doctrine. Special attention is given to the positive results of contemporary biblical studies for the understanding of Mary, the Holy Spirit, and the Church.

TO
JOSEPH A. FITZMYER, S.J.
on his sixty-fifth birthday

with personal gratitude
for thirty years of close friendship

and

with a gratitude shared by many
for distinguished and faithful service
to biblical and linguistic scholarship,
to the church, the priesthood, and the Jesuits

Biblical Exegesis and Church Doctrine

Raymond E. Brown, S.S.

PAULIST PRESS
New York/Mahwah

Nihil Obstat:
Rev. Myles M. Bourke, S.S.L., S.T.D.
Censor Deputatus

Imprimatur:
Most Rev. Joseph T. O'Keefe, D.D.
Vicar-General, *Archdiocese of New York*

June 26, 1985

The Nihil Obstat and Imprimatur are official declarations that a book or pamphlet is free of doctrinal or moral error. No implication is contained therein that those who have granted the Nihil Obstat and Imprimatur agree with the contents, opinions or statements expressed.

Library of Congress
Catalog Card Number: 85-62046

ISBN: 0-8091-2750-4 (paper) 0-8091-0368-0 (cloth)

Published by Paulist Press
997 Macarthur Boulevard
Mahwah, N.J. 07430

Printed and bound in the United States of America

CONTENTS

PREFACE

The deliberations of the Second Vatican Council gave a strong ecumenical directive to Roman Catholics. Trying to be faithful to that directive, Catholic interpreters of the Bible have applied their research in a way that would assist Christians to grow together in an appreciation of what God has given in His biblical word. Since both the biblical and the ecumenical concentrations are somewhat new on the Catholic scene, inevitably some have not easily comprehended or digested their import. Conscious of that, in recent years I have concentrated in lecturing and writing on traditional Catholic concerns, showing how contemporary scriptural research can enrich our doctrinal heritage rather than threaten it. It is encouraging that many other Catholic biblical scholars are engaged in the same positive endeavor.

Because of my optimism about the beneficial contributions of the biblical movement fostered by Vatican II, I am still stunned each time I encounter a distortion of these contributions by intelligent Catholic thinkers. I am not a foolish optimist; and so I anticipate the presence of ignorance and closed-minded bigotry even in the church—my problem is with those who should know better. Distortions are not the peculiarity of the ultraconservative extreme of the Catholic spectrum; they are just as frequent on the liberal extreme. Even though neither extreme is necessarily bad-intentioned, their distortions must be refuted in order to assist Catholics who are seeking to understand modern biblical research.

This volume is the result of my recent reflections in both the above directions, positive and negative. The initial chapters attempt to explain clearly the importance of the historical element in contemporary scriptural study and how this can illuminate the traditional doctrinal attitudes of the Roman Catholic Church. The following chapters draw on some recent writers to show how both liberals and ultraconservatives have misunderstood the doctrinal import of biblical exegesis. Then, moving beyond general observations, I exemplify the particular contributions of scriptural investigation to a Catholic understanding of Mary, of the Holy Spirit, and of the church.

A fair amount of this material has never been in print before; some of it has but is now totally recast (see Acknowledgments toward the end of the book). I appended two chapters (dealing with the Shroud of Turin and with R. Laurentin's exegesis of the infancy narratives) which, while not directly relevant to the main issue of the book, may be of considerable interest to biblical "buffs."

I am delighted to dedicate this book to a colleague since the days of doctoral studies at The Johns Hopkins University in Baltimore in the mid-1950s, a very close friend in scholarship and in the priesthood who (if I do not embarrass him) may well be judged the most learned NT scholar on the American Catholic scene.

Raymond E. Brown
Union Theological Seminary (NYC)
Easter 1985

Chapter 1
HISTORICAL-CRITICAL EXEGESIS OF THE BIBLE IN ROMAN CATHOLICISM

Both elements in the designation "historical-critical" are important. Although it may seem obvious that one must deal seriously with *historical* factors involved in the Scriptures, an intensive historical approach is really a recent phenomenon. That the Bible is inspired with God as its author had seemed previously to make irrelevant such historical questions as: Was a given biblical book written at one time and by one author? What traditions or sources did the human author(s) draw upon? What was the author's background and point of view? What were the problems of his time and community, and how did they affect his work? Does his message agree with that of other biblical authors? Have there been additions and even corrections added since the principal author first wrote?

Still more recent is the concept that various types of *"criticism"* or analysis might help to understand the biblical book, even aside from historical questions. These would include an analysis of a book in terms of its form(s) or genre(s) or type(s) of literature—each form has its own patterns which give us probabilities in determining how a particular piece of literature developed and should be interpreted. A knowledge of how literary features function in narration, poetry, drama, etc., is useful, as is a close study of overall structure in a work. With composite works, the signs of disparate material help to show the history of composition. In studying various forms of the text of a biblical book, one must know something about the patterns of scribal copying—a copying that influenced the transmission of the text from the time it was written to our extant manuscripts. All these aspects of "criticism" affect how we read biblical books composed 2000 to 3000 years ago; and their implications are not to be easily dismissed even by someone who says, "I read the Scriptures simply to let God speak to me." Inevitably that reader will pose questions to the Scriptures, and both the questions that are posed and the answers that are found will be shaped by the time in which the reader lives. Every reader today, no matter how professedly "simple," is consciously or unconsciously shaped by attitudes reflecting a critical sense—the critical sense by which we judge all that is communicated by modern media. Assumptions about historicity or science *will* be made by a reader who has any form of general education; and a basic grasp of what is involved in "the historical-critical" reading of the Scriptures will prevent the assumptions or presuppositions from being naive.

In a sense, historical criticism was developed through the recognition that the biblical accounts describe things that "ain't necessarily so." By the late 1600s the French scholar Richard Simon was pointing out that Moses was not the author of the whole Pentateuch; this led to the recognition of differences in the accounts of the genesis of the world, of the human race, and of Israel. By the late 1700s differences among the Gospels were leading to the realization that Jesus in his lifetime was in some degree different from the full-blown scriptural portraits of him. Unfortunately, a tinge of skepticism and even of rationalism marred the work of many earlier historical critics who reduced the Bible to a fallible account of primitive religious beliefs. Thus a major issue has been the debate about how historical criticism is reconcilable with and even beneficial to a faith stance in which the Bible is venerated as the inspired word of God.

Roman Catholicism came to grips with this problem more slowly than some of the Protestant churches but has now approved historical criticism more officially than almost any other church. The first hesitant step was taken by Pope Leo XIII in 1893 who, although seeing dangers in the "higher criticism" of his era, recognized that the biblical authors had the scientific vocabulary and outlook of primitive times and so could not be easily invoked in the modern debates about science—a statement with obvious implications for the whole creation/evolution discussion.[1] Much change in church thinking occurred in the next 75 years before Pope Paul VI in 1968 could firmly laud critical scholars of the Bible: "It

---

[1]Encyclical *Providentissimus Deus* (*RSS* #122; DBS #3289).

is your honor that you dedicate yourselves in a professional and scientific way to employ all the means given you by modern technology in the literary, historical, and archaeological fields, and to use them in order to increase our knowledge."[2] The history of this change in ecclesiastical outlook has been narrated many times,[3] but for the purposes of this chapter and this book let me concentrate on *the two basic steps* taken by Rome that led Catholicism away from a literalism or fundamentalism about everything described in the Bible. These two steps made it official church teaching that the whole Bible is not history and the Gospels are not necessarily literal accounts of the ministry of Jesus.

The first step was made in the 1944 encyclical of Pope Pius XII, *Divino Afflante Spiritu,* with its insistence that there are different literary "forms" in the Bible.[4] The Bible may be said to be a library (of Israel and of the church);[5] so that historical writing is only one part of the larger collection which includes poetry, drama, epic, parable, preaching, etc. This principle has implications for the factual questions which will surely be asked by inquisitive minds: Was Jonah really swallowed by a large fish? Were there magi who came from the East to Jerusalem because they saw a star that symbolized the birth of the King of the Jews? One cannot answer such questions simply by saying: "Yes, that is what the Bible says." Nor can one answer such questions by stressing inspiration. The issue is whether the inspired section of the Bible that reports such an event is inspired parable, or inspired history, or a type of inspired literature that lies between history and imaginative presentation. The determination of history in the Bible, like the determination of history in other ancient literature and libraries, thus becomes a much more complex task.

Even after the guidance laid down by Pius XII another step needed to be taken, for the historical truth of the Gospels remained a particularly sensitive issue. Under Pope Paul VI in 1964 the Roman Pontifical Biblical Commission tackled that problem with a subtle answer, replete with

---

[2]Address to OT experts on April 19, 1968 (*OCTBI* #993).

[3]Article "Church Pronouncements" in *JBC* 72:3–9.

[4]Paragraphs 35–39 (*RSS* #558–60).

[5]Vatican Library address of Pope Paul VI on March 25, 1972: "The Bible is not just a book; it is a library in itself, a set of books of every different literary genre" (*OCTBI* #1036).

implicit and explicit qualifications.[6] The basic thrust of the response is that, while the Gospels are substantially historical, they are not literally historical in every word and detail. Before being written down, the gospel material passed through three stages of development which thoroughly modified it: (1) Jesus did and said things (2) which eyewitness disciples later incorporated into their preaching, and (3) still later this preaching became the source of the writers who gave us the Gospels.

Each stage in this process had its own goal and its own modality. *First,* Jesus himself spoke and acted in the context of his own place and time. I have often sought to express this concretely by insisting that people take seriously that Jesus was a Palestinian Jew of the first third of the first century—a limitation that curiously seems to offend some. *Second,* the apostles adapted Jesus' message to the people of their time (the second third of the first century), an adaptation involving translation into another language (Greek) and an effort at comprehensibility in other circumstances (the large cities of the Roman Empire). Moreover, they brought to the memories of what Jesus had said and done the transforming enlightenment of their post-resurrectional faith in Jesus. *Third,* from the preaching the writers or evangelists (who may have been composing their works 10 to 30 years apart in different areas) selected stories and sayings that fitted their purpose in presenting Jesus to audiences of their time (the last third of the first century, for most scholars). Accordingly, they reorganized the material so that often it was presented more logically than chronologically; and they expanded it through necessary clarifications. None of this development need be seen as a distortion if it be remembered that the Gospels were not written simply as records to aid remembrance but as encouragements to belief and life. The historicity of the Gospels, then, is that of preaching, faithfully transmitting a message.

This explicit teaching of the 1964 Biblical Commission document, which in a brave but positive way affirmed that the Gospels are not necessarily literal accounts, had two implicit corollaries that have often been missed. Although the document refers to the Gospels as a whole, it is clear on careful reading that those who composed it were thinking only of that part of Jesus' activity for which the apostolic preachers were witnesses, namely, the public ministry from the baptism to the resurrection.

---

[6]The crucial section of the document may be found in *BRCFC* 111–15.

That the historicity of the narratives of Jesus' birth and infancy was another matter was understood by the Biblical Commission which planned but never completed a further study. The historicity of the infancy narratives has remained a debated subject among Catholic scholars, but occasionally one encounters a naive attempt to solve it on the basis of the 1964 statement which dealt with a section of the Gospels for which much clearer witness was assured. Secondly, although the Biblical Commission's statement (and the Vatican II document on Divine Revelation which used the Commission's statement as a guide) allows continued respect for the ancient terminology of "apostles and apostolic men" in reference to the Gospel writers, the Commission made a clear distinction between the apostles who preached and those who wrote the Gospels in dependency on that preaching. Implicitly, then, the Commission allowed for the view of most scholars today that no one of the evangelists was an eyewitness of the ministry of Jesus. Rather the evangelists were "second-generation" Christians drawing their knowledge from the earlier apostolic generation that had seen him and had shaped the tradition. This clarification does not undermine the value of the Gospels but explains their wide variations in reporting sequence and locations for which the evangelists had no personal remembrance. (By way of example, if the evangelists were not apostolic eyewitnesses, it is far easier to explain how Matthew's Gospel could report the cleansing of the Temple at the end of the ministry and John's Gospel report it at the very beginning.)

These developments in the Catholic approach to Bible historicity have beneficially effected an intelligent understanding of the Scriptures. Much less time and effort has been wasted on a fundamentalist attempt to defend every detail and to explain away every historical difficulty. More attention has been given to the purpose of the author, and a greater realism has marked our understanding of how Christianity grew and adapted to challenges. Of course, with a departure from absolute historicity, there is always the danger of moving too far in the other direction of minimalizing historical content. Yet relatively little of that has occurred among Catholic biblical scholars. Having found church authority a help in changing previous positions, they were not "angry young men" launching out on a crusade to overthrow. The best-known Catholic NT scholars in the world today would be regarded as moderates or centrists by their Protestant colleagues (who would have practical knowledge of radicalism and would be able to detect it).

HOSTILITY TOWARD HISTORICAL CRITICISM

Granted these facts of church support and of caution shown by Catholic biblical scholars, one may well be puzzled by occasional references to historical criticism as barren, passé, and wrong, at times accompanied by the glib assertion that the historical-critical approach is now questioned by "many scholars." With the understanding that the term "revisionism" can describe an effort to prove that the majority view of an issue is wrong, let me examine the various motives behind the revisionist attempts directed against the historical-critical method that is so widely attested in Catholic scholarship today. I shall separate the revisionists who reject or challenge historical-critical exegesis into two major groups.

I. Revisionists of a Literalist or Fundamentalist Tendency

(1) *Those who are annoyed by biblical criticism because it underlines the human elements in the Bible,* i.e., that the biblical books were written at a particular time, under particular circumstances, and in historically-conditioned language and outlook. As pointed out above, this issue is the heart of the whole historical approach to the Scriptures. Rejection of historical criticism on this score reflects a fear that biblical critics detract from the divine authority of the Bible. If the rationalist originators of historical criticism did not respect sufficiently the "of God" element in the Bible, the literalist rejectors of historical criticism do not respect sufficiently the fact that human beings spoke and wrote the "word" element of the Bible. I would maintain, however, that the weakening of either element in the "word of God" destroys the essential two-fold character of the Scriptures.[7]

Most Catholic readers of the Bible have had little training in this whole question of criticism. Because in the past the Bible has been very conservatively treated in the Catholic Church and because of influence from media fundamentalist preaching, they will tend to assume that everything described in the Bible actually happened. The first step in education may be the insistence that it is now perfectly correct within

---

[7]See a discussion of this in "The Human Word of the Almighty God," *CMB* 1–22.

Catholic teaching to recognize that not everything in the Bible is historical.

Another step is to acquaint Catholic readers with the rationale behind the historical-critical questions that scholars ask, especially if those questions are *prima facie* disturbing. There is no way to prevent ordinary people from becoming aware of the kinds of questions that are being asked in scholarship today; for, whether the scholars consent or not, their views are picked up by the media and often sensationalized. The instinctive reaction of many Catholics will be annoyance at the presumption of the scholars unless somehow they can see that scholarly probing is approved by the official church and is not threatening to faith. For instance, scholars have asked whether a star really shone in the East to reveal to magi the birth of the King of the Jews, a star that came to rest over a house in Bethlehem. One must consider whether such questioners are rationalistically denying the miraculous or simply examining whether the infancy narrative of Matthew necessarily belongs to the same category of developed eyewitness tradition that is involved in Matthew's account of the public ministry. A decision that the infancy narrative belongs to some other literary form which allows a freer use of OT symbolism may cause the scholar to think that the star need not be a historical phenomenon. The decision is not a matter of rationalism and lies perfectly within the lines of investigation encouraged by church authority.

Inevitably, it will be objected that such a historical-critical approach takes away from the absolute authority of the Bible. But Roman Catholics have traditionally insisted that biblical authority comes to expression in the context of the believing and teaching church. Some Catholic defenders of biblical literalism would impose attitudes more often associated with ultraconservative Protestants who deny the need for an interpreting church. If everything in the Bible is not necessarily historical, Catholics are *not* left without the guidance of the church as to what they must believe. This last observation brings me to a second type of literalist revisionist.

(2) *Those who claim historical-critical exegesis leads to a denial of Catholic dogmas.* "Fundamentalism" is a term that had its origins among Protestants who saw biblical literalism as the only way to preserve certain fundamentals of the Christian faith, and some Catholics

continue to promote literalism for the same reason. Let me make three observations in reference to this issue. *First,* in Catholicism dogma expresses divine revelation as interpreted by the teaching church. Therefore, it is perfectly possible to claim that the Bible, historically-critically considered, does not offer sufficient proof for a doctrine and still think the dogma must be accepted as infallibly taught because of church tradition. Sometimes such an approach has been dismissed as fideism. It would be fideism if one held that the church teaching was to be maintained even though the biblical evidence denied the dogma, or if there was no intelligible argument for a position of the church which goes beyond the biblical evidence. But in the examples I am thinking of, Catholic exegetes are not suggesting that the limited biblical evidence contradicts church dogma or that the church has no reason for going beyond the biblical evidence. They are simply placing the responsibility for the dogma where it belongs, not in the Scriptures, but in the complementary developments of subsequent church tradition—developments that stem from reflection upon the Scriptures in context of church life. Nothing in these remarks suggests a theory of "*two* sources of revelation": the basic witness to the Christian revelation is the tradition of the church, but NT Scripture represents only the first-century phase of that tradition. (I shall develop this point in Chapter 2 below.)

Second, one must be precise about what is Catholic dogma and what is popular understanding of that dogma. In other words, one must distinguish between a nuanced and a naive presentation of the dogma. It is now official Catholic teaching (*Mysterium Ecclesiae* [1973]) that frequently doctrine has been phrased in "the changeable conceptions of a given epoch" and that one must distinguish between the truth infallibly taught and the way that truth has been phrased.[8] I would maintain that there is *no irreconcilable conflict* between the results of Catholic historical-critical exegesis and a nuanced understanding of Catholic dogma. Rather, literalists who attack such exegesis as undermining the faith are often identifying the dogma with their own naive understanding of it. For instance, there is a Catholic dogma about God's creating the world, in the sense of God's bringing the world into being by His absolute power;

---

[8]The crucial section of this document may be found in *BRCFC* 116–18. For further discussion on this point, see pp. 28-29 below.

but there is no Catholic dogma about how creation took place, or how long it took. There is a Catholic dogma that bishops are the successors of the apostles, in the sense that the pastoral care of the churches once exercised by the apostles ultimately passed into the hands of the bishops; but there is no Catholic dogma that the Twelve Apostles laid hands on immediate successors appointing one bishop in each church. Many more examples of the distinction between nuanced and naive understandings could be offered; and in each of them it would be the naive understanding, which is not really part of the dogma, that is being challenged by historical-critical exegesis.

Third, one must be very accurate in reporting the precise results of Catholic historical-critical exegesis. I think I have a reasonably good grasp of what the best-known NT exegetes propose in reference to the virginal conception of Jesus, the bodily resurrection, the divinity of Jesus Christ, Christ's founding the church and instituting the sacraments, the position of Peter in reference to the later papacy, etc. In no instance do *most* Catholic historical-critical exegetes contradict Catholic dogma properly understood. I do not mean that there is not an occasional Catholic NT exegete, for instance, who denies the virginal conception or the bodily resurrection. I judge, however, that this is a minority view, to be traced not to historical-critical exegesis as such but to one person's practice of that exegesis—a practice that I regard as incorrect. I do not mean that there are not Catholic systematic theologians who deny church dogmas, citing historical-critical exegesis as support for their position. In such instances, however, one must be very careful to ascertain whether they cite *Catholic* exegetes and cite them *correctly.* (Chapter 3 below will be devoted to a detailed discussion backing up these general observations.) Conservative critics may wish to hold Catholic exegetes responsible for the misuse of their exegesis by others, but that is pure nonsense: the misuse of a discipline never vitiates the discipline.

If one takes into account the three points I have just made, one will realize that the underlying dislike of historical-critical exegesis in this type of revisionism is related to the effect that such exegesis has in making one rethink Catholic dogma, as to what is the core of the dogma and what is the time-conditioned expression of it. That rethinking produces uneasiness on either end of the Catholic spectrum. Historical criticism should not be made to pay the price for those who have their own axes to grind.

II. Revisionists for Hermeneutical Purposes

There is a type of revisionist who does not espouse a fundamentalist or literalist approach either to the Bible or to doctrine, but who has another set of interests in relation to the Bible, interests to which historical criticism may seem an obstacle. Once again, there are subdivisions:

(a) *Those who have found biblical criticism barren,* providing little results for spirituality, preaching, or theology. Protest is sometimes raised against a biblical criticism that is totally immersed in recondite historical questions or in attributing verses to sources so that it overlooks the living word of God. A more nuanced evaluation faults biblical criticism because its practitioners make no relationship between their research and theology or church life. Yet, in point of fact, today historical critics often do *not* confine their overall studies (as distinct from highly specialized articles or monographs, which remain essential) to source analysis or to nontheological interpretation of the text. Increasingly, commentaries and topical works written by exegetes seek to understand the whole world of thought (historical, comparative, ideological, sociological, religious) that comes to light in the biblical text. Stereotypes of biblical criticism, based on rationalist efforts of the 19th century, are increasingly unfair; for historical critics do not do their duty if in interpreting a religious text they do not show what it meant religiously to those who wrote and read it. True, theological categories discovered by biblical critics may not be the same as those of systematic theologians, but the proper relationship between the discoveries of the biblical critic and the world of the systematic theologians is often between two different theological interests rather than between the nontheological and the theological. Surely, more needs to be done in discovering how these two different theological domains, biblical and systematic, are related; but there is far less cause for despairing that the twain will never meet.

Thus the overall charge that historical criticism is barren is overdone; and the proper remedy for whatever truth there may be in the charge is to join to historical criticism spiritual concerns, theological interests, and indications on how to preach from the Bible. No one with a proper sense of hermeneutics claims that historical criticism is the only or the total approach to the Bible. It is an even greater exaggeration, however, to claim that spiritual, theological, and preaching interests can dispense with the contributions of historical criticism—that attitude creates the danger of building castles in the air. Above all, historical questions must be answered by historical means. The biblical opinions of Church Fathers or spiritual writers are extremely valuable to the development of overall Catholic thought; but unless those writers had historical information they cannot answer historical questions. The effort of a few in their rhetorical overkill to demean historical criticism because it is not all-sufficient represents a danger of the recrudescence of the disdain for the historical that has too often marked theoretical thought.

(b) *Literary critics who insist that biblical works, once written, have a life of their own,* so that questions of sources, author's intention, and community setting become irrelevant. Similar reactions may come from the advocates of structuralism or semiotics more concerned with the inner structure of the text than with the author's background. A type of revisionism related to such interests might ignore historical questions as totally useless to interpretation. (A strange hybrid is René Laurentin's recent work on the infancy gospels which I shall discuss in Chapter 4 below: he promotes semiotics but is intensively interested in historical issues which he solves not by historical criticism but often by pious assumptions. Therefore I classify his revisionism under I rather than under II.)

Here less arrogance is necessary on both sides of the question. Many historical critics understand well that their work grasps only part of the meaning of the text, precisely because that text has its own identity as a body of literature and as a section of the larger canon of Scripture. I stressed this strongly in *CMB* (esp. pp. 23–24) even as I was ardently defending the importance of biblical criticism. There I insisted that hermeneutics or the discovery of biblical meaning goes beyond historical criticism and that the historical critic has no reason to denigrate the importance of contributions from other forms of hermeneutical investigation. But on the opposite side, the advocates of other types of biblical criticism (literary criticism, narrative criticism, rhetorical criticism, structuralism, etc.), despite their enthusiasm at the novel insights gathered by their methodologies, should also learn modesty. Too often a new approach is hailed as dispensing with all that has gone before instead of adding to what has gone before. No matter what import these other approaches may have, there is *one question that will always be fundamental:* What was the biblical author trying consciously to communicate to his readers and how did those readers grasp what he wrote? Obviously we have only limited means to discover that, but any approach which ignores it wanders too far from our basic criteria of meaning.

In this light I want to add a particular comment about "canonical criticism," particularly as phrased recently by B. S. Childs.[9] This criticism involves a recognition that the NT books as they left the quill of their authors did not stop their theological journey. The canon is the normative collection of Scriptures, which in the case of the NT reached its most widely accepted form in the 4th century. The canonical process may be seen as the collecting, ordering, and transmitting of the tradition which had been phrased in first-century writings in such a way as to enable that tradition to function as Sacred Scripture for a community of faith and practice (Childs, 25). The process was not uniform or unilinear, but involved a basic continuity between the early stages of NT formation and the effecting of an authoritative collection. It loosened the individual texts that constitute the NT from their first-century historical setting and enabled them to address every future believer—a reinterpretation for new situations that involved considerable freedom (Childs, 23). This means that paradoxically "the witness of Jesus Christ has been given its normative shape through an interpretative process of the post-Apostolic age" (Childs, 28). All this I agree with, having written myself strongly in the same direction in *CMB* 23–44. *Biblical* hermeneutics or the search for the meaning of the *Scriptures* cannot be content with the literal sense (the meaning that the book had when it was first composed); it must look to the meaning that the book had when it became scriptural or part of the Bible, i.e., part of the canon.

Nevertheless, the issue remains about the role given to a search for the literal sense in such a larger hermeneutical process, a search that

---

[9]*The New Testament as Canon: An Introduction* (Philadelphia: Fortress, 1985). Childs is wide-swinging in his critique of contemporary NT exegetes. Theorists (and abstract critics) of hermeneutical method should be forced to write a substantial commentary on an individual biblical book, so that by their fruits, and not by their theory, they can be judged. Few are as brave as Childs in doing this. Others can evaluate the OT commentary he produced (and that is his field of expertise); his suggestions about the NT are often so lopsided that they could produce commentaries with insufficient relation to what the biblical author intended.

heavily involves historical criticism. Theoretically Childs does not deny the importance of historical criticism; it is "here to stay" (Childs, 45). Practically, however, in his evaluation of NT exegetical commentaries, Childs decries any priority given to the literal sense and deplores the attempt to distinguish between the literal and canonical levels of meaning pertinent to the Bible. Thus, for instance, in Childs' view the historical situation faced by the author of I John becomes totally subordinate to the fact that the church has read this letter as a universal or catholic epistle to all Christians (Childs, 487). The search for canonical meaning becomes almost the sole goal of the interpreter. I agree that the canonical meaning of Scripture is more normative for Christian living; but the biblical scholar (in a role distinct from the role of church preacher and teacher) must uncover the literal sense in order that the ancient dialogue which took place in the canon-forming process—the dialogue between the particularistic first-century meaning and the more universalistic later meaning—may remain open. Through the universalizing thrust of the canonical process, the Scriptures became "a living vehicle through which the Lord of the church continued to address his people" (Childs, 29). But how do we stop the church insight from being frozen when the canon was substantially formed (4th century) or at any other moment, thus terminating the dialogue? How do we make certain that the Scriptures remain "a word from the ever-present Saviour," and not the church talking to itself? And since the NT text of this "word" was written in the first century, how do we stop a church interpretation from becoming so free that really another "word" has been substituted and the continuity of the process broken? Historical-critical exegesis in its quest for the literal sense is an ally in preventing such abuses. It does not give us the normative sense of Scripture but challenges the church by its discoveries (which change and grow as the techniques of investigation improve). The literal sense serves as an obstacle toward substituting a self-composed word for the word given so long ago. Childs (47) agrees with me that the essence of canon is a fundamental dialectic between what a text meant and what it means. Alas, by sending the exegete almost exclusively to search for the canonical meaning, he tends to obliterate the importance and distinctiveness of the literal level uncovered by historical exegesis. In his method, what it meant will soon no longer be able to speak to what it means.

My final word, then, in reference to the importance of other forms of criticism is the insistence that historical criticism must be allowed to make its major contribution toward answering the question of biblical meaning. The maxim of Pope Pius XII (*Divino Afflante Spiritu* 23 [*RSS* 550]) remains valid: "Let the interpreters bear in mind that their foremost and greatest endeavor should be to discern and define clearly that sense of the biblical words which is called literal."

(c) *Those who seek to use Scripture in support of a cause.* Sometimes advocates of particular causes can be quite vituperative about historical criticism as distracting from a hermeneutic or principle of interpretation more relevant to the cause they are advocating. Liberation theologians often think that the issue of the oppressed and poor is the only optic through which Scriptures may be read; accordingly, they may look on the majority of exegetes as remote from the real issue of the Third World and as oppressors who are depriving the readers of the Bible of a cutting tool for societal change. Feminists may argue that historical-critical exegesis is an instrument of a patriarchal scholarship insensitive to the women's movement. There have been Marxist interpretations of Scripture—again, quite different from the results of historical-critical exegesis.

A modern issue may well raise important questions that have been neglected in previous exegesis and thus enrich scholarship. For instance, when biblical scholars are asked to study about the oppressed, or about women, they sometimes discover in the text aspects previously overlooked. Often, historical-critical study is an effective tool in working out such new insights, so that there need be no contradiction between this form of exegesis and "relevant" issues. On the other hand, a monolithic attempt to make the Scripture serve one modern cause may easily become counterproductive and lead to a distorted eisegesis, i.e., reading things into the text. Rightly, complaints have been raised against an older proof-text optic whereby a doctrine became the eyeglass through which Scriptures were read, and passages were sought out that might be ingeniously interpreted in support of that doctrine, no matter what the original author meant. Prooftexting in support of modern causes is just as one-sided; and historical-criticial exegesis may be a healthy antidote in reminding us that the biblical authors were often ignorant of, or uninterested in, issues that seem important to us. That does not make those issues less important, but it sets them in the context of history. If some issues that mattered to Paul or Matthew (like the Jew-Gentile conversion matter) seem irrelevant to us today (even when interpreted intelligently as to their underlying significance), that may constitute a salutary warning that our burning issues may seem irrelevant several decades or a century from now. A Scripture read solely through the modern-issue optic could also seem irrelevant in the future.

*   *   *

As a conclusion to my remarks about the various forms of biblical revisionism hostile to historical-critical exegesis, let me make the following observations. The number of such revisionists is small, despite attempts, mostly by ultraconservatives, to make it seem a vast movement. The demise of historical criticism is "exaggerated," as Mark Twain observed upon reading his own obituary. The various revisionists who work from very different principles might dislike one another's exegesis even more than they dislike historical-critical exegesis, so that the revisionist movement is not of one mind. Imagine what strange bedfellows the fundamentalists I have discussed under I above would make with the liberationists and feminists described under IIc.

One thing that many of these revisionists have in common is their dislike of a relatively unimpassioned, hard-headed look at history, a look that seeks to serve no particular cause. (I recognize that no scholarship is totally objective or disinterested, but in principle historical criticism tries to be descriptive.) If this outlook on history is *contemptuous* of interests foreign to the historical-critical discipline (dogmatic, spiritual, social, literary, etc.), then the historical-critical discipline is being poorly practiced. But, if *without contempt,* historical-critical exegesis shows that the interests of the original author were different from what we might have expected, the resultant dialogue with those who would use the text for their own interests can be fruitful in keeping the use both sober and balanced. No other method has been devised that will answer purely historical questions better; and we are on dangerous ground when we decide that historical answers (even when they are disturbing) are irrelevant or must be changed precisely because they upset our outlook. Once again, I am not saying that historical answers need tyrannize our views so that our views of present realities are incorrect because they do not agree with past views of that reality. I am insisting that our views will be stronger and more persuasive if we have not sought to bend the past to suit us, but have entered into dialogue with past contributions to the total picture.

The future lies not with a rejection of the historical-critical method (which I regard as a permanent contribution to human knowledge), but in a refinement of the method, so that it will answer appropriately posed questions even more accurately, and its contributions to the larger picture of biblical interpretation can be seen in better perspective.

Chapter 2
CRITICAL BIBLICAL EXEGESIS AND THE DEVELOPMENT OF DOCTRINE

Having discussed the necessity and importance of historical criticism in the first chapter, I now turn to the relationship of critical NT studies to official church teaching. Before I illustrate various ways in which the church has moved from the NT period (as constructed by scholars today) to its developed doctrine, let me state my presuppositions.

PRESUPPOSITIONS OF THE DISCUSSION

If one defines a centrist position as what is taught and accepted in the main institutions of Catholic learning, then just as biblical criticism may be described as centrist, so also may the position that the church can teach infallibly certain doctrines. I am perfectly aware that Hans Küng has challenged the notion of infallibility; but even before his positions were declared irreconcilable with holding a Catholic teaching office, they were widely challenged, by very reputable and competent Catholic theologians. Therefore I would judge that Küng's position has relatively little following in the Catholic mainstream. Rather than spending time on defending the possibility of infallibility, I wish for my discussion to emphasize two aspects of infallibility.

The first involves the discernment of which doctrines are taught infallibly by the church. Too often, ordinary Catholics resort to their catechisms as a guide to the church's teaching, not realizing that traditional catechisms can cover a whole range of information, running from pious practices to doctrine taught by the highest church authority. Even collections of the teachings of the Catholic Church, listing statements of councils, popes, and Roman commissions, do not distinguish between infallible teaching reflecting divine revelation and various lesser forms of authority and admonition. (Ultraconservatives love to cite against biblical and theological scholars the *Syllabus of Errors* published by Pope Pius IX in 1864, without alerting their followers that the most authoritative collection of church documents felt compelled to preface the *Syllabus* with a note stating that the value of the individual "erroneous" propositions varies considerably.[10]) There exists no universally accepted list of all the doctrines taught infallibly by the Roman Catholic Church. Realistically, no great problem of identification arises when doctrines are proclaimed officially by the *extraordinary magisterium* of the church, e.g., a doctrine defined by a creed or an ecumenical council or a specific papal statement (the Immaculate Conception and the Assumption). The delicate area is where we lack such definitions and must depend on the constant, regular teaching of the church (the *ordinary magisterium*). Such teaching often does not specify whether what has been universally and constantly proposed for belief is an intrinsic constituent of divine revelation; and so there can be honest dispute among theologians, none of whom are rebellious against church authority, over the infallibility of doctrines in this category.[11] Even when church authorities ultimately intervene in such a dispute, most often they do so by insisting that the doctrine must continue to be taught, without clarifying the infallibility status. I felt that it was necessary to give this caution as a preparation for what will follow in this chapter, even though most examples of infallibly taught dogma that I shall use below are not disputed.

---

[10]DBS p. 576.

[11]In *VCBRJ* 35 I stated: "I think that according to the usual criteria applied in Roman Catholic theology the virginal conception would be classified as a doctrine infallibly taught by the ordinary magisterium." I felt obliged to point out that other theologians do not agree on the infallible status of this doctrine and that there are some difficulties about the history of the doctrine. The very fact that I listed some of the problems and that I consistently repeat "I think it is infallibly taught," and do not state "It is infallibly taught," seems to infuriate some ultraconservatives. In my judgment only the pope and the bishops have ultimate authority to say, "It is infallibly taught" when one is dealing with an issue of the ordinary magisterium. But, as I have pointed out before (*BRCFC* 12–14), some pretend to a doctrinal authority that goes beyond that of pope and bishops.

Moreover, even if one or the other of my examples is questioned, the general issues of relationship to NT thought remain valid.[12]

Another important aspect of infallibility concerns the formulations in which the church expresses its doctrine or dogma. Much of what follows will concern how in its infallible teaching the church goes beyond the NT—a development that does not invalidate dogma. Unwittingly, an impression may be created that the church can define whatever it wishes and cannot be challenged constructively by scholarly finds. Throughout the discussion, however, I shall insist that a doctrinal trajectory should be traceable from the NT outlook to the later dogma, even if the connection between the two goes beyond pure logic. Here let me devote some consecutive remarks to the limitation of dogmatic formulas and thus indicate an area in which there can be a constructive challenge to the usual understanding of a doctrine—a challenge often based on a more perceptive reading of Scripture. Precisely because the emphasis in chapter 1 on historical-critical exegesis stresses the human elements in the NT witness to revelation, we must not underestimate the human elements in the vocalization of divine revelation by the later church.[13] A glimmering of an official acknowledgment of the historical conditioning of dogma came in the speech with which Pope John XXIII opened the Second Vatican Council:[14] "The substance of the ancient doctrine of the deposit of faith is one thing, and the way it is presented is another." But a clear affirmation came only a decade later in a document where one might least expect to find it—the declaration of the Doctrinal Congregation (Holy Office) refuting Hans Küng's challenge to infallibility.[15]

---

[12]The same may be said of my exegesis: even if one or the other point I make is questioned by *reputable* biblical scholars, the general issues I am discussing remain valid. Exegesis has never been able to give absolutely certain results, but that does not liberate theologians from considering seriously the results produced by the best exegesis of the times. Those who complain about the uncertainty of modern exegesis sometimes have a romantic notion that the exegesis of the past was *not* uncertain and give undue reverence to dubious views simply because they were held in the past.

[13]We have moved beyond the Reformation battles which accepted the "sure" word of the Scriptures but disputed whether church traditions were divinely guided or merely human. There is a human element both in the Scriptures and in church traditions, but that prevents neither from serving as an authoritative witness to God's revelation.

[14]*DVII* 718.

[15]*BRCFC* 116–18.

This very careful document accepted the principle of the historical conditioning of dogma in four ways: (1) the meaning of the pronouncements of faith depends partly on the expressive power of the language used at a certain point in time and in particular circumstances; (2) sometimes dogmatic truth is first expressed incompletely (but not falsely), and at a later date receives a fuller and more perfect expression; (3) the church usually has the intention of solving certain questions or removing certain errors, and these things have to be taken into account in order that the pronouncements may be properly interpreted; (4) sometimes the truths enunciated by the church magisterium are in terms that bear the traces of the changeable conceptions of a given epic. This means that some doctrinal formulas may give way to new expressions which, proposed and approved by the sacred magisterium, present more clearly or more completely the same meaning.

The language of the Roman decree is stilted, but the implications are clear. Even though we may insist that a doctrine is infallibly taught by the church, that doctrine is historically conditioned and may have to be reshaped as we come to perceive more fully just what issue really was at the heart of the divine revelation and how much of the way in which that issue was once formulated represents changeable conceptions. Certainly one of the major factors that can lead to reformulation is biblical investigation which shows us that the grasp of Scripture inherent in the ancient formulation of a dogma did not always coincide with what the biblical author originally intended. A better understanding of NT contentions may lead to the sharpening of dogma—but, and this is the point of the church warning against Küng, not to the invalidation of dogma. I would ask the readers to keep these observations very much in mind as I proceed to stress the importance of church doctrine and the right of the church to move beyond the Scriptures. My stress does not mean that the church formulations are exempted from being answerable in some way to the Scriptures. One must always keep in tension two extremely important affirmations from the Dogmatic Constitution on Divine Revelation (*Dei Verbum* 3:10) of Vatican II: ''The task of authentically interpreting the word of God, whether written or handed on, has been entrusted exclusively to the living teaching office of the church'' and ''This teaching office is not above the word of God but serves it, teaching only what has been handed on.''

THEORIES RELATING SCRIPTURE TO DOCTRINE

In the "olden" days (before Vatican II) it was apparent, even against the background of a sometimes unsophisticated biblical exegesis, that certain doctrines of the Roman Catholic Church were not easily detectable in the NT. In a widely held thesis of two sources of revelation, *Scripture and Tradition,* it could be maintained that such doctrines were passed on orally as part of the living tradition of the church, and were simply not mentioned until a much later era because no one questioned them. A more nuanced thesis was that such doctrines could be logically derived in an almost syllogistic manner from ideas or affirmations that were in the Bible. Vatican II changed the focus of the discussion significantly. The draft of the schema on the sources (plural) of revelation, submitted to the Council in November 1962, was rejected; and in the process of recasting there emerged from the Council an approach wherein *Scripture was seen as part of Tradition*[16]—the tradition of Israel and of the early church. Therefore most theologians no longer speak of two sources, and indeed, the whole language of sources probably should be overhauled. The one source of revelation is God Himself; what we are really discussing is the witness (or witnesses) in which the human expression of that revelation is to be found. At most, we can speak (in the plural) of the sources of our knowledge of revelation, or sources in which revelation comes to expression, not sources of revelation.

Increasingly, too, doctrines for which there is no sufficient witness in the Bible are dealt with in another manner. A more sophisticated theory of hermeneutics argues that the written books of the Bible, as literary artifacts, had a life of their own and so their "meaning" involves the ongoing interpretation of them within the Christian community (see p. 21 above). A distinction has sometimes been proposed between what the human author of the Scriptures understood and what God intended when He inspired that author *(sensus plenior).* While something can be said on behalf of such a distinction, too often it has been understood in a rather mechanical manner.

When all is said and done, however, our fathers and mothers in the

---

[16]The Pontifical Biblical Commission document of 1964 (footnote 6 above) speaks of Gospel formation in terms of "the three stages of tradition by which the doctrine and life of Jesus have come down to us."

faith and in theology were, in my judgment, not foolish in the problem they perceived. Even with a sophisticated theory of hermeneutics it is still legitimate to ask what a human author intended when he wrote at a particular moment in time, or what his readers understood when his writing was first presented to them. How is what we may call in an abbreviated way this "literal sense" of the Scriptures related to the dogmas of the later church—dogmas of the 4th, the 13th, the 16th, or the 20th century? Was a dogma that was proclaimed only in those later centuries already in the mind of the biblical author as he composed his book and, in particular, as he composed a passage which subsequent theology has related to that dogma? Occasionally, practitioners of a sophisticated hermeneutics claim that the mind-set of the original author is irrelevant and that the real question is whether his work was patient of the dogmatic interpretation given to it by the later church. But in a divided Christianity people are going to be interested in the mind of the original author, no matter what subsequent generations may have found in his work. Pope Pius XII was very wise in affirming the primary importance of discerning the literal sense (p. 23 above).

EXAMPLES OF VARIOUS RELATIONSHIPS BETWEEN SCRIPTURE AND DOCTRINE

In this chapter I am going to suggest that the relationship between the mind-set of the NT authors and the dogmas of the later church is varied and complex. Without attempting to be exhaustive I shall isolate three different relationships, and for each I shall offer concrete examples.

I. Doctrines for which There is Abundant but Incipient Basis in Scripture

Let me use the Trinity as the first example to illustrate what I mean by this relationship. Three different figures, Father, Son, and Spirit, are brought into conjunction in the NT. Some NT formulas join the three; other references unite the Father and the Son; and still other references relate the Spirit to the Father and/or to the Son. Nevertheless, in no NT passage, not even in Matt 28:19 ("Baptizing them in the name of the Father, and of the Son, and of the Holy Spirit") is there precision about three divine *Persons,* co-equal but distinct, and one divine *Nature*—the core of the dogma of the Trinity. Greek philosophy, sharpened by continuing theological disputes in the church from the 2nd to the 5th centuries, contributed to the classical formulation of the dogma. On the one hand one may say, then, that the precise trinitarian dogma is not detectable in the literal sense of the NT, i.e., was not observably understood by first-century authors and audiences. On the other hand, reflections on NT texts played a crucial role in leading the church to the dogma of three divine Persons and one divine Nature, a dogma that employed new terminology and embodied new insights as a response to new questions. There is no need to posit new revelation to account for the truth ultimately phrased in the trinitarian dogma, since that truth was already revealed when God sent Jesus Christ and when the risen Christ communicated his Spirit. Yet the development was not simply a matter of logic. In faith, one can claim that the Spirit guided the church as it moved from the NT triadic passages to perceiving and proclaiming the trinitarian dogma. Christians should not be embarrassed to affirm that they depend upon the Spirit's guidance in such an essential dogma, for that guidance is really an application of Christ's promise to be with his community and to send the Paraclete to guide them along the way of all truth.

Let me append some observations that, although centered on the trinitarian dogma, will apply to other examples I shall mention below. In discussing how the church moved from the NT to its dogma of the Trinity, some may prefer to speak of "tradition" being the guiding factor. I have no objection provided that "tradition" is not understood in a static way (and indeed provided that it is seen as another name for what I am trying to describe more fluidly). If "tradition" implies that first-century Christianity already understood three coequal but distinct divine Persons and one divine Nature but simply had not developed the precise terminology, I would dissent.[17] Neither the terminology nor the basic ideas had reached clarity in the first century; problems and disputes were

---

[17]The early Newman had almost this sense of tradition, suggesting that *homoousion,* "one in being," was "almost found in Scripture"; but the later Newman was much more subtle about tradition. See J. Pelikan, *The Vindication of Tradition* (New Haven: Yale, 1984) 29–40; G. Biemer, *Newman on Tradition* (New York: Herder and Herder, 1967) 33–67.

required before the clarity came. But, as we can see from the NT, some first-century Christians did have views about the *pre-existent* divinity of Jesus and *personal* characteristics of the Spirit—elements that established a line of development attractive to later church teachers when they finally formulated the trinitarian dogma.[18] There was a distinct element of the new, but the new in continuity with the old. Precisely because the "trinitarian" line of development was not the only line of thought detectable in the NT,[19] one must posit the guidance of the Spirit and an intuition of faith as the church came to its decision. The liturgy, the prayer life of the faithful, and the *consensus fidelium* would have all contributed to this intuition. Emerson's plea for "a poetry and philosophy of insight and not of tradition"[20] would make no sense in my understanding of the role of tradition in the development of doctrine, for tradition would embody insight, offering it a nourishing matrix. And if one reflects on the presupposition I made on pp. 28-29 above about the ongoing dialogue between Scripture and church teaching, it will be seen that, in my judgment, even when finally fixed in a formula, tradition does not stifle further insight derived from a deeper penetration of Scripture.

In terms of ideational and terminological development from NT to church dogma, the concept of "sacrament" is somewhat similar to that of the Trinity. In Reformation debates there arose the issue of how many sacraments were derivable from the NT: two, three, or seven. However, if one wants to be exact in historical-critical exegesis, the NT never uses the term "sacrament," nor any other common term to describe the actions that Christians regard as sacraments. Certainly the NT mentions baptism and eucharist but never joins them together under one "umbrella" term.[21] There are also references to a prayerful anointing of the

---

[18]The Fathers at Nicaea were perfectly aware that in the way they were defining the divinity of Jesus they were going beyond purely biblical categories, and Athanasius insisted that the issue was whether they were being faithful to the direction of Scripture ("Letters concerning the Decrees of the Council of Nicaea," esp. 5.19–21 [*Library of Nicene and Post-Nicene Fathers*, Series 2, 4.162–64]).

[19]Passages such as Mark 13:32; Luke 2:40,52; Heb 5:8, indicating limited knowledge and the necessity of learning, and John 14:28; Mark 10:18, suggesting that Jesus was less than God the Father, were used against the developments of Nicaea.

[20]Discussed by Pelikan, *Vindication* (footnote 17 above) 65ff.

[21]Even in later history baptism and the eucharist had different theological treatments.

The issue was really that the biblical term was ambiguous while the new biblical one wasn't

sick (connected with the forgiveness of sins) and public confession of
sins by Christians; but these actions are not related to baptism and the
eucharist. Therefore, the development of a common term and a common
concept ("sacrament") for uniting such diverse actions goes beyond the
NT and would have to be understood once more as a Spirit-guided insight
into basic relationships among sacred actions familiar to early Christians. Also, the exclusion of other actions from this category, e.g., the
washing of the feet (which in John 13:8,14 is ordered by Jesus under pain
of having no "portion" with him) represents a selection that cannot be
explained by simple logic; it reflects the church's innate ability to determine what is essential in God's plan for its existence. Here, of course,
liturgical practice would be very important. Christians baptized and they
celebrated the eucharist before any NT author wrote about those actions;
the liturgical practice continued after the pertinent NT passages were
written. This continued practice may have been influenced by the NT
references but had a dynamism of its own.[22]

There would be many other dogmas that could come under this first
type of development; but since this is the least problematic doctrinal development, let us turn to more difficult relationships between Scripture
critically examined and later church doctrine.

II. Doctrines for which There is Slender Basis in Scripture

In the developmental relationship just discussed there were numerous references to the three divine agents and to baptism and eucharist,
so that in the NT era, even if the dogmas of the Trinity and the sacraments were not known, presumably few Christians would have been totally ignorant of or opposed to the building blocks of such dogmas. We
now move to another category of doctrinal development where the basic

---

Tertullian's *De baptismo* was the first theological tractate on that sacrament (*ca.* 200) and
gave definitive guidance on many disputed issues. F. Cayré, *Manual of Patrology* (Paris:
Desclée, 1940) 2.382, calls the *De corpore et sanguine Domini* of Paschasius Radbertus,
written in 831, "the first scientific monograph on the Holy Eucharist"; and it opened centuries of acrimonious debate.

[22]Pelikan, *Vindication* (footnote 17 above) 9, points out the anomaly that radical Protestant scholarship finally came to understand the importance of pre-Gospel tradition (which
no longer exists) for an understanding of the Gospels but then proceeded to ignore the
importance of post-Gospel tradition (which exists in thousands of volumes).

ideas are not widely attested either in most NT books or in all NT decades. Let me begin with the virginal conception.

In my own writings and those of many other scholars, there is ample documentation that, while a high christological evaluation of Jesus as Son of God or Lord is found throughout the NT, there is no unanimity as to which phase of Jesus' career was connected with this identification. There are sayings in the NT that have Jesus being named ("made," "declared," or "hailed as") Son of God, Lord, or Christ in reference to his parousia (Acts 3:20; I Cor 16:22) or to his resurrection (Acts 2:32,36; 5:31; 13:33; Philip 2:9; Rom 1:4). Certainly the three Synoptic Gospels are written from the viewpoint that Jesus was Son of God throughout his public ministry, as declared firmly by a divine voice at the baptism. John's Gospel is written from the viewpoint that Jesus was the divine Word uttered before creation. But in only two places in the NT is there a connection of the identity of Jesus as the Son of God with his conception, namely, chap. 1 of Matthew and chap. 1 of Luke. In both these instances the identification is made in relation to Mary conceiving Jesus in her womb through the Holy Spirit without male intervention. In my judgment, and in that of most other scholars, both authors literally intended a virginal conception (even though their primary interest may have been christological). There is no other clear reference to the virginal conception of Jesus in the NT, despite elaborate but unconvincing efforts to find it in Paul (Gal 4:4), in Mark (6:3: "son of Mary"), and in John (1:13, read with a singular subject). There is no evidence, of course, that any NT author denied the virginal conception; but silence where it might have been appropriate to mention the virginal conception suggests that many did not know this facet of Jesus' origins.

In subsequent centuries up to the 19th, with rare exception,[23] there was virtual Christian unanimity that factually Mary conceived as a virgin. Such a physical fact was implied in the creedal proposition "born of the Virgin Mary," for, although primarily christological and not physiological, this statement presupposed physical virginity. Despite some modern claims to the contrary, I think the majority of Roman Catholic theologians would agree with me that the virginal conception is a doctrine infallibly taught by the Church's ordinary magisterium.[24] How does

---

[23]See *VCBRJ* 47–52.

[24]See footnote 11 above. *VCBRJ* 23–26 listed some exceptions; John L. McKenzie

the church move from the evidence that in the NT only two evangelists mentioned the virginal conception and the likelihood that it was known to a minority of NT Christians to an affirmation that the historicity of the virginal conception is part of the divine revelation about Jesus Christ? Some revisionists will dismiss the modern critical perception of the NT as skeptical or rationalist, but most who choose to wrestle perceptively with the problem of doctrinal development will deem it irresponsible to abandon an approach every time it uncovers disconcerting data.

No doubt in times past the fact that the virginal conception was found in inspired Scripture would have settled the issue; but the Roman Catholic Church has now taught officially that inspiration cannot be equated with historicity (pp. 15-16 above), and so the possibility must be envisioned that the infancy narratives are an inspired form of literature in which all details are not historical. Some may argue that the alternatives to virginal conception are not tolerable in Christian thought. But theologians have asked why is it not tolerable to think that Jesus might have had a human father—would that make him any less the eternal Son of God from all eternity? Why is it so intolerable to think that Mary and Joseph conceived Jesus in wedlock—would that make Mary any less holy? Less convincingly some have asked whether it is intolerable to think that Jesus was conceived out of wedlock—would that not be in harmony with his role as the most rejected of men? And if one responds that Christian thought has firmly rejected anything of sin in relation to Jesus (a rejection that would presumably affect his origins as well), a modern feminist might describe Mary as the victim of male lust and power and thus far from sinning in conceiving Jesus out of wedlock.

Yet despite all these possibilities the Roman Catholic Church has continued firmly to maintain that Jesus was conceived of a virgin without human father.[25] Some will dismiss that as a narrow conservatism, but

seemed to deny the virginal conception when he reviewed my *BM;* and now Jane Schaberg has published a feminist book, *The Illegitimacy of Jesus* (Minneapolis: Winston, 1985), obviously positing a human father.

[25]The fact that I think this is so has not prevented me from discussing the issue as objectively as I am able; for in *VCBRJ,* esp. 38–47, I showed that some of those who accept the virginal conception do so for the wrong reasons. In my judgment the theses that Jesus would not be the Son of God and that Mary would not be holy if Jesus were conceived in wedlock through relations between Joseph and Mary must be resisted even by those of us who accept the virginal conception.

those of us who judge it to be infallible teaching must recognize that something other than sufficient biblical evidence[26] or logic or strict theological reasoning is at work. From living with the image of Christ, proclaiming him, celebrating him in liturgy, and growing in the understanding of essentials about him, the church through its official teachers has made its decision that a minority NT view, however scarcely attested, was a true evaluation of what God did in Jesus. His beginnings on this earth reflected his identity: *human* because of the womb of Mary, *divine* by a creative action of the Spirit similar to the creative act described in the first book of the Bible—an act that brought human life itself into being. In so proclaiming, the church which gave birth to the NT has affirmed the instinct of many NT writers that Genesis supplies the true comparison for the awesome importance of what God did in bringing His Son into the world.

Something similar probably occurred in relation to the bodily resurrection of Jesus. There is far more NT attestation for the resurrection of Jesus than for the virginal conception; but not all the attestation makes it clear that the resurrection meant that Jesus' body did not corrupt in the tomb. In general, for Jews, bodily resurrection meant the emergence of a body from the place in which it had been laid to rest;[27] yet the Jewish thought of resurrection, since it included those long dead, would involve corruption of the non-skeletal parts of the corpse. That this corruption did not occur in the instance of Jesus Christ may be seen from the Gospel

---

[26]In *VCBRJ* 66 and *BM* 527 I stated that the scientifically controllable evidence derived from a study of the NT left the historicity of the virginal conception unresolved—the ecumenical book *MNT* came to the same conclusion on pp. 291–92: "The task force agreed that the historicity of the virginal conception could not be settled by historical critical exegesis." (Each time I have complemented my statement with the judgment that biblical criticism *favored* the historicity of the virginal conception and that infallible church teaching could resolve the ambiguity left by historical criticism.) Those who have asked whether I was looking for the scientific evidence of a medical examination have failed to understand that "scientific" is applicable to historical research in a broad sense of verifiable evidence, not in the narrow sense applicable to physical, physiological, and mathematical studies. To illustrate my point, I can say of the death of Jesus on the cross what I cannot say of the virginal conception: Scientifically, the controllable evidence derived from a study of the NT establishes beyond reasonable doubt that Jesus was crucified—and this without a medical exam.

[27]The Jewish view of resurrection is complex, however; see P. Perkins, *Resurrection* (Garden City, NY: Doubleday, 1984) 37–56.

narratives of the empty tomb,[28] but is not clear from most other NT passages. Nevertheless, in teaching about the resurrection through the ages, the church has consistently presupposed that Jesus' body did not corrupt in the tomb, whether that was challenged by ancient Jewish opponents, or by Christian docetists, or by modern skeptical theologians. Therefore, personally, I would judge that the *bodily* resurrection is infallibly taught by the ordinary magisterium, and that, while there may be debate about the nature of the transformed resurrected body, Catholic teaching does not permit one to maintain that the body of Jesus corrupted in the tomb.[29] Such a doctrine does not involve fideism but the acceptance by the church of some NT voices as representing an authoritative insight into the resurrection of Jesus, over against the silence of other NT witnesses about the bodily component and about non-corruption. (In this case, however, I would insist that silence really tells us little about the knowledge of those other NT authors, whereas I think that much of the silence concerning the virginal conception betrays ignorance.) Once again no simple doctrine of inspiration can be invoked in settling the issue; nor can the argument that the alternative to non-corruption is theologically repugnant. Theology-library shelves are filled with works by theologians who proclaim their belief in Jesus' divinity and his victory over death but do not think that either doctrine has anything to do with the non-corruption of his body.[30] Once again those of us who accept the church's guidance on this issue as an infallible interpretation of revelation have to posit a penetration of the mystery of Jesus Christ, this time not in ref-

---

[28]That on the grounds of the lateness of the empty-tomb *narratives* one cannot easily dismiss an early tradition that Jesus' tomb was empty I have argued in *VCBRJ* 113–25. See now J. L. Craig, "The Historicity of the Empty Tomb of Jesus," *NTS* 31 (1985) 39–67.

[29]Please note how carefully I phrase this in terms of non-corruption. I hope that my writings show that I have no simplistic understanding of the physicality of Jesus' resurrection. On the other hand I have little tolerance for "brave" assertions by theologians, e.g., "My faith would not be shaken if they found the skeleton of Jesus in a tomb in Palestine." More to the point is whether such a discovery would have shaken the faith of the apostolic preachers upon whom Christianity depends. Let me state boldly: there is no evidence whatsoever that any in the NT who considered themselves Christians thought that Jesus' body could still be moldering in the grave.

[30]Although Perkins' *Resurrection* (footnote 27 above) is an exegetical study, she enters into dialogue with some modern theological views of victory over death.

erence to the beginning of his earthly career but to the conclusion of it. Perhaps the non-destruction of Jesus' body is seen by the interpretative intuition of the church (under the guidance of the Spirit) as an important key to the renewal of the world at the end of time and to the final mystery of the resurrection of the dead. The latter is proclaimed in the creed by the church, without indulging in any literalist description or explanation;[31] yet it seems to involve a future hope that goes beyond being with Christ after death: the saints *are* with Christ, but their bodies *will be* raised.[32] The church may be intuiting that a belief in a resurrection of Christ which has as an essential component the non-corruption of his corpse in a tomb is the essential forerunner to belief in God's eschatological action in raising the dead.

Let me mention still another example of the development of dogma from a relatively few NT witnesses—the development of the papacy and the Petrine succession, as it is related to NT passages that give Peter a unique role in the Church (Matt 16:18; Luke 22:31–32; John 21:15–17). To treat the dogma of the papacy would require a long treatment but let me quote the USA Lutheran-Catholic dialogue on the key point:[33] "There is increasing agreement that the centralization of the Petrine function in a single person or office results from a long process of development. . . . The Catholic members of the consultation see the institution of the papacy as developing from the New Testament roots under the guidance of the Spirit. Without denying that God could have ordered the Church differently, they believe that the papal form of the unifying ministry is in fact, God's gracious gift to His people." Understandably the Lutherans did not see themselves bound by this Catholic insight, but dialogue was facilitated because Catholics did not attempt

---

[31]If in my judgment careful NT exegesis supplies a corrective to liberal theological assertions about the resurrection of Jesus, it also supplies a corrective to fundamentalist or ultraconservative literalism about the resurrection of the dead at the end of time.

[32]In conversation with a Catholic theologian who does not believe in the bodily resurrection of Jesus, I asked what was the difference between Jesus' victory over death and the victory of a saintly Christian. He responded, "Jesus was the first to conquer death." I would maintain that the NT indicates something quite different: the resurrection has taken place for Jesus; it has not yet happened for the saintly deceased Christians.

[33]*Papal Primacy and Universal Church,* ed. P. C. Empie and T. A. Murphy (Lutherans and Catholics in Dialogue V; Minneapolis: Augsburg, 1974) p. 19, #21.

to read the developed papacy back into the NT era and did not pretend
that the development of the doctrine was simply an issue of inexorable
logic.

I have given three examples (namely, the virginal conception, the
bodily resurrection, and the papacy) where I think the development of
doctrine consists in deciding which NT voices, among different voices,
should be taken as an authentic guide to what is essential in Christian
faith. I am sure that there are many more examples; for, as modern scholarship becomes more precise about the diversity of biblical voices, the
fact that the church is often being selective when it speaks definitively
on issues will become more apparent.[34]

III. Doctrines about which the Scriptures are Virtually Silent

I now move to a more difficult area where, instead of a few NT
voices, there is virtual NT silence on a subject that has later come to be
regarded as a matter of Catholic faith. Let me take as the first example
the continued virginity of Mary. If Matthew is specific that Joseph did
not know Mary until the child Jesus was born, no NT author ever tells
us whether or not Mary and Joseph had marital relations after the birth
of Jesus. Of course, there is no reason why a NT author should have told
us of this, and we are not certain that any NT author was in a position
to have knowledge on this issue. We have no right in a serious discussion
to invoke as conclusive the completely unestablished thesis that Mary
lived on in the Jerusalem community and shared her most intimate se-
crets with the early Christians. The last mention of Mary in the NT story
is *before* Pentecost in the Book of Acts, and everything else about her
subsequent career is pure guesswork. In reference to the perpetual or
continued virginity of Mary after the birth of Jesus, pertinent NT data
are the references to the brothers and sisters of Jesus in Mark 6:3; Matt
13:55–56; and to the brothers in Acts 1:14; John 2:12; 7:3, along with
the Pauline reference to James as the brother of the Lord (Gal 1:19).

---

[34]The NT voices to which the church has not given preference when it formulated
doctrine are not thereby to be considered silenced or useless. My book *The Churches the
Apostles Left Behind* (New York: Paulist, 1984, esp. pp. 148–50) was written to show how
the voices which have not had preference can often serve as a corrective to exaggerations
which have sprung from the choices the church has made.

Since the normal Greek word for blood-brother and blood-sister is used (and Greek does have vocabulary for other more distant relatives, such as cousins) and since the brothers are most frequently shown in the company of Mary, it would be usual to assume that these were Mary's other children born after Jesus, her firstborn.[35] Nothing in the NT would clearly contradict that; and certain church writers, including Tertullian, affirmed that Mary had other children.

Nevertheless, in a series of debates ranging from the second to the fourth century, the church (West and East) took a definitive stand that Mary remained a virgin physically through all her human life. The church never defined just what relationship to Jesus was held by those whom the NT calls "brothers" and "sisters"; nor did the church claim that it had identifiable testimony establishing that Mary and Joseph had no marital relations after the birth of Jesus—a fact that goes beyond the identity of the so-called brothers and sisters. (It would have been possible for Mary and Joseph to have had relations whether or not they had any more children, and the knowledge about the lack of further relations would have been a much less public item.) How has the church come to this knowledge which it now, according to most theologians, proclaims as a matter of Catholic faith? That issue has special importance because in the last few centuries many Christians, heirs of the Protestant reform, deny that Mary remained a virgin, even though the great reformers, Luther, Calvin, and Zwingli, all affirmed the perpetual virginity of Mary.

There have been elaborate Catholic treatments of the few texts of the NT that have any pertinence to the issue, but in my judgment, the most they have succeeded in proving is that the NT does *not* affirm that the brothers and sisters were children of Mary.[36] (That may seem little,

---

[35]It is true that the Hebrew and Aramaic words for brother and sister cover a wide series of relationships, extending beyond children of the same parents. But in interpreting Greek writers one does not resort to the import of underlying Semitic terms unless there is a reason to do so. That reason is supplied primarily by later church tradition about Mary's perpetual virginity, not by the NT.

[36]Three affirmations should be kept distinct. First, the NT tells us that Mary had other children; that is false. Second, a *prima facie* reading of the NT would make one think that the brothers and sisters of Jesus were Mary's children if one did not have tradition to the contrary; that is true. Third, since there is a tradition to the contrary, it is not unscientific (footnote 26 above) to invoke complicated NT crossreferences and Semitic vocabulary to argue that the "brothers" of Jesus were not Mary's children; that is true, as recognized by the ecumenical book *MNT* 292.

but I think the affirmation that the Scripture does not teach the contrary is an exceedingly important component of the development of doctrine.) For the church to come to an affirmation of the perpetual virginity of Mary, did it need a privately preserved body of information, inevitably stemming from Mary herself, that there were no marital relations? Factually one cannot prove such information and theologically I see no need of it. The perpetual virginity of Mary has customarily been linked with her response to the great gift of the conception of God's Son. Her decision to remain a virgin, following the annunciation, was seen as a fitting response to that gift; and so one may speak of a church analysis of the mystery of Mary and her role in the plan of salvation. We spoke of the church penetrating the mystery of grace-giving actions in church life (the "sacraments"); so also by living with the image of Mary and reflecting on her relationship to Christ, the church could have come to a factual statement about a facet of Mary's career after the birth of Jesus— the ongoing virginity—precisely because this facet was seen to be meaningful in church life.[37] Evidently this reflection on Mary in terms of perpetual virginity began early. In the 2nd-century *Protevangelium of James* Joseph is portrayed as an old man who had children by a previous marriage when he married the very young Mary. Despite the name "James" (the "brother" of the Lord who would have known the family history) most of the *Protevangelium* is clearly fantastic fiction. But the story enshrines a series of perceptive intuitions interpreting NT data: Mary conceived as a virgin (and there were no subsequent marital demands since Joseph was elderly); Joseph was not on the scene during the ministry (he had already died); there are children related to Jesus usually found in Mary's company (she was raising her deceased husband's offspring); they were called brothers and sisters of Jesus (because Joseph, who was thought to be the father of Jesus, was their father). Later the Western Church abandoned this explanation by following Jerome's theory that the "brothers and sisters" were Jesus' cousins. This shift was

---

[37]The perpetual virginity of Mary has also been wrongly used by some to disparage the sanctity of marital relations. Realization of that fact may make it easier for Catholics to understand that Protestants who think that Mary and Joseph had other children in wedlock after the virginal conception of Jesus are not dishonoring Mary. With Jesus, John the Baptist, and Paul all celibate, if Mary remained a virgin, most Christians (for whom marital relations are an expression of the holiness of their state in life) have no major NT model of family existence.

a vivid demonstration that the church was not tightly controlled by family information, any more than it was shaped by scriptural passages establishing perpetual virginity.[38] It had a basic intuition about Mary that was dramatized in different genealogical theories explaining away the "brothers" (West: cousins; East: earlier children of Joseph).

I think other instances of movement from the silence of the NT to doctrinal affirmation may be found in the Immaculate Conception and the Assumption. I do not find a single text of the NT that in its *literal sense* refers to either of these two dogmas. There are texts, of course, that refer to Mary as most holy among women and especially blessed by God, but there is nothing in those texts that specifies the unique blessing of her being conceived without original sin or being assumed bodily into heaven. In the case of the Assumption, since the last mention of Mary is before Pentecost, the NT tells us nothing about her death and its aftermath—nor is there a really reliable early tradition on the Assumption. (The Assumption, if taken to mean that Mary did not corrupt in the grave, has at least a somewhat observable component when compared with the Immaculate Conception, which is, of course, completely unobservable.) The likelihood that a private tradition about these doctrines passed down from Mary to the defining church is very small. The clear concept of original sin comes in the 4th century,[39] and therefore it is extremely unlikely that Mary could have phrased her privilege in terms of a deliverance from original sin. A discernible orthodox tradition about the Assumption, stemming from eyewitnesses of Mary's grave, simply does not exist in the first centuries. (Early references are involved with a theory about the assumption of John, the son of Zebedee, which in turn is tied in with the Encratite heresy of opposition to marriage, praising John as a virgin.)

How then did the Roman Catholic Church move toward the definition of such doctrines, granted the silence of the NT? Once more, I

---

[38]The thesis that Luke 1:34, "How can this be since I do not know a man?", should be understood as an intention or a vow to remain a virgin ("How can this be since I shall not know a man?") was rejected by the ecumenical scholars in *MNT* 114–15, even as I rejected it in *BM* 303–9.

[39]The concept that all human beings come under the guilt of a sin other than their actual sins goes beyond Rom 5:12 where "all men sinned" seems to refer to actual sins. Christian reflection on Romans and Genesis led to the development of a doctrine of original sin which in the West found its chief expositor in Augustine.

would maintain that the doctrines stem from a reflection on the role of Mary in salvific history. The reflection took place in prayer, liturgy, popular imagery, and theology; the underlying role had its roots in the NT. Mary is portrayed by Luke as the first one to hear the gospel about Jesus, Son of God, son of David; and she responds to this gospel by the fundamental attitude of a disciple: "Be it done unto me according to Your word" (Luke 1:38). Therefore Luke portrays Mary as the first Christian disciple—an analysis that has won ecumenical acknowledgment by both Protestants and Catholics.[40] Deliverance from what the Western church has called "original sin"[41] through the death and resurrection of Christ has been recognized in theology as a fundamental privilege of all those who become Christian disciples by hearing the gospel and accepting it through faith and baptism. In saying that Mary was the first Christian to be delivered from this universal sinfulness (indeed, even to the extent that she was *conceived* free from sin) is in a sense saying that the first Christian disciple was the first one to receive the privileges of discipleship. Similarly, resurrection of the dead to blessedness at the end of time is a promise held out to all Christian disciples as part of the heritage of believing in Christ.[42] To say that Mary was assumed into heaven[43] is to say that the eschatological resurrection anticipated for all Christians was first given to the first disciple. A thesis positing that, despite the silence of the NT on the Immaculate Concep-

---

[40]*MNT* 126, drawing on the observations of the Finnish Lutheran scholar, H. Räisänen. I shall return to this aspect of mariology at the end of Chapter 5 below.

[41]Eastern Christianity did not develop this concept under its Augustinian modality, and modern theologians have sought to rethink the doctrine. Nevertheless, the concept of a sinfulness that touches the whole human race, independently of an individual's personal sins, is a firm part of the Christian heritage, quite apart from the theory that the race had a single parentage or that the sin was passed on through concupiscence to all the descendants of a single set of parents. In fact, the Augustinian concupiscence theory hindered the development of the doctrine of the Immaculate Conception, since Mary was conceived through the intercourse of her parents who presumably had feelings of desire. The East may be said to have had the substance, if not the precise imagery, of the doctrine of the Immaculate Conception: the unique and unmatchable holiness of Mary, not tainted by sin.

[42]See my remarks above on p. 39 about the relationship of Christian resurrection to Christ's resurrection.

[43]To be precise the definition by Pope Pius XII did not state that Mary died, but death and resurrection are assumed by most theological reflection on the Assumption. The very old tradition of the "dormition" of Mary points in this direction.

tion and the Assumption, the Spirit has led the church to penetrate the
salvific significance of Mary as first Christian is a far safer approach than
attempting to find dogmas in NT passages where the authors show no
consciousness of them. Of course, once having defined the Immaculate
Conception and the Assumption, the church has cited certain biblical
texts as illustrating the dogmas; but that is often simply free application.
The issue I am discussing in this chapter is the relation of dogmas to what
the NT meant to the people who wrote it and first read it—an issue of
acute concern in theology and ecumenics—and there is no evidence that
any NT author thought of the Immaculate Conception and the Assumption.

*　　*　　*

I would like to turn now to another form of silence in the NT,
namely a *partial* silence affecting a crucial aspect of a later doctrine.
Paradoxically, as we shall see, this partial silence may be more difficult
to deal with than complete silence.

A fundamental part of the definition of a sacrament is "institution
by Christ." Catholic theologians know well the difficulty of relating all
seven sacraments to statements or deeds whereby Jesus would have
shown an intention of founding or establishing an on-going sacred action. Nevertheless, baptism and eucharist have usually been agreed upon
by both Catholics and Protestants as two sacraments for which NT institutional statements or actions are the most clear. Modern biblical criticism, however, creates problems about the specific institution even of
these two.

There is little evidence that Jesus baptized during his ministry: the
Synoptic Gospels are totally silent on the subject, and the statement in
John 3:22 that Jesus did baptize is offset by the affirmation in John 4:2
that he did not. Two passages are often looked on as possible instances
of the institution of baptism. First is Jesus' statement to Nicodemus in
John 3:3,5 about the necessity of being begotten from above (or born
again) of water and spirit. It would be very difficult, however, to affirm
by modern critical rules that in its present form this is a historical statement of Jesus during the ministry. Secondly, the institution of baptism
has been connected with the post-resurrectional directive in Matthew
28:19, "Make disciples of all nations, baptizing them in the name of the

Father, and of the Son, and of the Holy Spirit." Yet the absence of such
a command in the other Gospels[44] and the seeming ignorance of this directive among early Christians, both in terms of baptizing in the triadic
formula and of a mission to the Gentiles, causes critical scholars hesi-
tation.[45] A moderate biblical criticism, with which I would associate myself, would maintain that the Matthean text is an ecclesiastical
interpretation of the mind of Jesus—an inspired interpretation but one
that reached clear formulation decades after the resurrection. Obviously
there might have been other words of Jesus about baptism which, although not recorded in the NT, influenced church practice. But on the
basis of the only NT evidence we have, it would be unwise to interpret
the institution of baptism by Christ to mean that in his lifetime Jesus specifically commanded the practice. Rather, baptism may have been a
practice that developed very quickly in the church in imitation of Jesus'
own baptism by John because it was *thought to be loyal to Jesus' own
attitudes.* Thus the doctrine of "institution by Christ" remains valid but
is understood historically in a more subtle way as the church's interpreting the mind of Jesus.[46]

The significance of this sacramental institution issue for the development of doctrine becomes clearer when one thinks of the eucharist.
The three Synoptic Gospels and Paul agree that on the night before Jesus
died he took bread and wine and interpreted them in terms of his own
body and blood. In two of the four accounts (Luke 22:19; I Cor 11:24,25)
he is recorded as directing his disciples to do likewise in memory of him.
Probably the majority of biblical critics would regard this directive as a
later liturgical specification similar to the baptismal directive "Make dis-

---

[44]Somewhat parallel is Mark 16:16; but that belongs to the Marcan Appendix, a later
addition to Mark that may be posterior to Matthew.

[45]A historical evaluation of words spoken by the risen Jesus is difficult; see *CMB* 13–
14.

[46]It is important to note that the church speaks of institution by Christ and not institution by Jesus. "Christ" becomes a substitute name for "Jesus" after the resurrection,
as Christians begin to identify Jesus in a role perceived in faith. On the one hand, the church
is not necessarily proclaiming an institution during Jesus' earthly life; on the other hand,
it proclaims that the sacraments are not mere human conventions and that they are part of
God's plan in Christ.

ciples of all nations, baptizing them in the name of the Father and of the Son and of the Holy Spirit''—in other words, a recognition that the practice of the eucharist was according to the mind of Jesus and following out his intention. Even if one argues to the contrary that Jesus *did* speak the words, ''Do this in commemoration of me,'' at the Last Supper, modern critics would be very hard put to determine how definite was Jesus' knowledge of the future and whether he foresaw a long period before the end of time in which the eucharist would be celebrated frequently in his memory.[47]

The related issue of the priesthood needs to be treated even more circumspectly. There is no evidence in the language of Jesus that he thought about a priesthood replacing the Jewish priesthood in the Temple. He had disciples and seemingly sent them out on mission; among the disciples he called the Twelve to sit on twelve thrones judging the twelve tribes of Israel; but he designated none of his followers as priests. Nevertheless, later church reflection has found in the eucharistic action at the Last Supper, and in the directive in two of the four accounts, ''Do this in commemoration of me,'' the institution of the priesthood. Once more our evidence points to a process of development.[48] Certainly there were eucharists in the early Christian communities; and although we have practically no information about how those eucharists were conducted, it is not unlikely that someone presided at the eucharist and spoke the eucharistic words. We have virtually no information in NT times about who this person was or how the person was designated to do this. I emphasize ''virtually *no information.*'' Often those who begin reading modern treatments of the priesthood become quickly aware that the older

---

[47]See ''How Much Did Jesus Know?'' in my *Jesus God and Man* (New York: Macmillan, 1967) 39–102. The verse that follows the eucharistic words in Mark 14:25; Matt 26:29, where Jesus says that he will not drink of the fruit of the vine again until he drinks of it anew in the kingdom of God, does not seem to posit a long future of eucharistic celebrations.

[48]Although the power of priestly sanctifying was given by God in and through Jesus, it took time for Christians to see that this power was exercised in the eucharistic table-meal, since their Jewish heritage would have caused them to associate sacrifice and priesthood with actions done in the Temple by those of levitical descent. A further step was to confine the exercise of this priestly power to the bishop and presbyters who administered the community.

view that the apostles themselves ordained all the ministers of the eucharist cannot be verified in the NT;[49] but sometimes they remain unaware that more "liberal" claims are equally unverifiable. For instance, the statement of E. Schillebeeckx in his book *Ministry* (New York: Crossroad, 1981) 30, "In the house churches of Corinth it was the hosts who presided at the eucharistic meal," is an overstated guess (see below p. 122). No matter what one may theorize, we simply do not know, even if both conservatives and liberals seem compelled to overcome ignorance by assurance. Eventually, presiding at the eucharist became the exclusive prerogative of the bishop. That had already happened in some of the churches addressed by Ignatius of Antioch; and by the latter part of the second century this seems to have been virtually the universal practice. If the bishop were not present, he could designate others to preside; and eventually, as dioceses grew, it became the custom for the presbyter of the local area, rather than the bishop, to preside at the eucharist.

Working with the little evidence we have, we might *posit* a development in which there was a gradual regularization of those who could be presiders until the ordained clergy alone had that role, and a gradual designation of that clergy as priests. All of this would be related to the eucharistic action of Jesus at the Last Supper, and to an increasing understanding of the eucharist as sacrifice. In this development, the institution of priesthood by Christ would have to be understood as a complicated historical process that began at the Last Supper. One would *not* need to think that, as Jesus reclined at that meal, he had clearly thought out the continuing eucharists of the church and those who would preside at them. In my judgment, such a view in no way weakens the validity of the dogma of Trent (DBS 1752) that "Christ" established the apostles as priests with the words "Do this in commemoration of me." It simply demands nuance:[50] namely, that establishment by Christ involves looking at what Jesus did historically on the night before he died in the light of the christology, liturgy, and ecclesiology of the next 100 years which interpreted the original action and words.

---

[49]See *PB* 5–45.

[50]The demand for nuance is misrepresented by some ultraconservatives as undermining the value of dogma. Rather it prevents the humanly conditioned *expression* of dogma from being elevated to divine revelation.

THE IMPORTANCE OF UNDERSTANDING DEVELOPMENT CRITICALLY

In this brief survey of the way in which doctrine has developed beyond what the NT authors and audiences would have understood, I have treated only about ten dogmas under three categories. A more ample treatment would discover many other variations of development. But let me leave that task for someone more competent. I want to terminate this chapter by stating why I think the issue important. If in some way, however untechnical, we can manage to communicate to our Catholic people that the relationship between our dogmas and the NT situation is not simple, I think we gain some very positive benefits over an older view that the dogmas of the church could have been affirmed in the NT era if only someone asked about them. Let me enumerate the gains.

First, as I suggested in Chapter 1, despite attempts at revisionism, modern NT criticism with its component of historical sensitivity is not about to pass away. Sooner or later those who receive an extended formal education will be made aware that the dogmas taught in their catechism are not to be found so simply in the NT. Unless we have at least prepared students in some way for this observation, the discovery can easily lead to a loss of faith. Misunderstanding the dependency of dogma on explicit NT knowledge, they will reject dogmas because they now know some of the complications of the NT situation.

Second, in an increasingly pluralistic world, Roman Catholics are constantly in dialogue with other Christians (as well as non-Christians) who do not accept defined Catholic dogmas. If Catholics think that holding a dogma involves finding it with clarity in the NT, they are bound to think that those who do not find it are dishonest, or rationalists, or irreligious. An understanding of the complicated aspects of the development of doctrine will, at least, make more intelligible why other Christians or outsiders do not accept some doctrines that Catholics accept. More often such non-acceptance is not because they are dishonest, or skeptical, or irreligious, but because they do not attribute to the church the same authority that we attribute.

Third, and most important, this understanding of doctrinal development makes very clear the centrality of the church in the proclamation of the Gospel. If by logic, or sheer historical reasoning, or traceable eyewitness tradition, the inevitable necessity of many dogmas *cannot* be shown from the NT data, we must then recognize that the guarantee about what must be believed and proclaimed rests with the Spirit working in the Church and speaking through its teachers. I would have thought that the Reformation struggles established clearly that Roman Catholic faith and practice are not confined to the affirmations of the NT era, but astoundingly this is now widely denied by both ultraconservative and liberal Catholics. For instance, in my books *VCBRJ* and *BM* I wrote that modern biblical criticism could not establish fully the historicity of the virginal conception (even though I found biblical criticism more favorable to historicity than to non-historicity) and that, accordingly, our acceptance of the virginal conception depends on the doctrinal teaching of the church. I was accused by ultraconservatives of fideism (p. 17 above) for accepting the doctrine when I declared (wrongly, in their judgment) that there was not sufficient biblical proof. I was accused by liberals of cowardice for not denying the doctrine when I correctly acknowledged there was not sufficient biblical proof. If this ultraconservative and ultraliberal attitude toward biblical research and development of doctrine is not remedied in some way, I fear that we may see an even more divided church and departures from the church.

Let me give a pastoral example. Two recent Popes, Paul VI and John Paul II, have taken a decisive position against the ordination of women. I suspect that the majority of theologians would not yet regard the church position on the issue as *de fide* even though the refusal would certainly have to be regarded as authoritative.[51] Let me try to treat even-handedly two possible contrasting future actions showing how either one could produce enormous division in the church. Suppose that in the next century a pope ultimately decided the long practice of ordaining only males was not a dogmatic stance but a matter of church organization, shaped in an era where the full potentialities of women's abilities and service had not yet been realized. And in this hypothetical (and perhaps quite unlikely) development, let us suppose that the Roman Catholic Church began ordaining women. I would suggest that a great number of

---

[51]A *de fide* teaching implies that God has revealed the truth; the church can take a stance on its own authority without invoking divine revelation. Then, however, the church also has the right to change an authoritative stance. Some years ago in *BRCFC* 47–50 I listed some problems that needed to be faced clearly in church discussion of this issue.

conservative Catholics would leave the church and form a schismatic communion. (Those who say that many women are leaving the church because no movement has been made on this issue often do not recognize how many people might leave the church if movement *were* made on the issue.) Their reasoning would be that Jesus did not ordain women and that therefore the church does not have a right to ordain women. This is not a guess: one finds this reasoning already in the ultraconservative press, with the writers rejecting the possibility of any new action by the church on a reading of the NT situation which simply assumes that the historical Jesus, in choosing men as the Twelve,[52] had thought about ordination, about future priests, and about the whole situation of ministry in a pluralistic society. Thus, if change were made, the contention that most or all dogmas were already formed in the NT period, including the dogma of the male priesthood, could lead to schism on the conservative side. If one could have a virtual schism over changing the Tridentine Mass, one can certainly have a schism over a much more radical step.

But let us also look at a possible reaction on the other side of the issue by supposing that popes in the 21st century continue the authoritative attitudes of Popes Paul VI and John Paul II in refusing to ordain women, ultimately making it a matter of defined faith that only males can serve as ordained ministers of the eucharist in the Roman Catholic Church. (Even those who do not think it a matter of faith now must recognize the reaffirmation in the new code of canon law: "Only a baptized male can validly receive sacred ordination" [1024].) I think there could be a schism by a number of liberal-minded Catholics who would reject this (hypothetical future) dogma on the grounds that Jesus had female disciples, that he never spoke about ordination, and that there were women heads of Christian households in NT times. They would argue that, therefore, the later church does not have the right to make a decision so definitively restricting the subject of ordination. The notion that a dogma which clearly goes beyond the NT era could be defined by the church might be rejected by the liberal even as it would be rejected by the ultraconservative.

I contend that the future of the Roman Catholic Church demands the clear and unwavering recognition of its right to teach definitively and

---

[52]One cannot assume that the choice of the Twelve to sit on thrones judging the twelve tribes of Israel (Matt 19:28; Luke 22:30) is the same as the choice of priests.

infallibly on matters not settled in the NT, and that therefore the argument about what was in the mind of Jesus will often not settle a modern
question. Please understand my full acknowledgment of the responsibility of the church to move in directions that are consonant with the
values of Jesus, according to Vatican II's statement that the church's
"teaching office is not above the word of God but serves it" (p. 29
above). For that reason I have no simple solutions about which way the
church should move on disputed modern issues. But Catholics must be
willing to live by the authoritative decisions of the church, even when it
goes beyond the Christianity of the apostolic era, whether the development was by historical specification or by penetration of meaning and
implication. I anticipate a liberal objection that, while one must be willing to accept what the church decides, the church does not consist solely
of the hierarchy. That is true, of course; but in a Catholic understanding
of faith no authoritative position can be fully binding without the component of the hierarchy. In fact, the final clarity of authoritative doctrinal
positions has frequently come through statements of the hierarchy in the
form of papal definitions and conciliar decisions.

I have given but one example (the ordination or non-ordination of
women) of how the failure to deal with doctrinal development could lead
to a rending of the church from either side. I do not think that this example is an exception. In most of the controverted issues of our time,
the decision taken will go beyond what was the clear position of Jesus
or of Christians in the NT era. (That will seem obvious to all Protestants
and Roman Catholics who have a critical view of the limitations of the
NT era.) Those who claim as their only authority Jesus or the NT,
whether they be ultraconservative or liberal, may well be in conflict with
the church that has to face problems Jesus never faced. Thus, I am re-
affirming the paradoxical position that only a nuanced view of development is really loyal to the best Catholic traditions and can preserve
Catholicism today. Neither a fundamentalist interpretation of the NT,
which finds later dogmas with great clarity in the NT era, nor a liberal
view, which rejects anything that goes beyond Jesus, is faithful to Catholic history.

Two quotations from prominent Roman Catholic figures embody
my message in this chapter. William Cardinal Baum, Prefect of the Roman Congregation for Catholic Education, stated in the Jan. 27, 1980
Washington Star: "The 'evidence' of Scripture—both to the scholar and

even to the believer—is *of itself,* inconclusive in determining the meaning of the most fundamental tenets of the Christian faith: the identity of Jesus, the meaning of his life and death, the nature of his triumph, the obligations imposed on his followers, the consequences of his life for us, etc.'' That recognition of the limits of the NT critically studied is complemented by the affirmation of Karl Rahner:[53] ''The Church cannot be a debating society: it must be able to make decisions binding on all within it. Such demand cannot be *a priori* contrary to man's dignity, if . . . he is indeed a social being. And then a supreme point at which all reflections and democratic discussions are turned into universally binding decisions cannot be without meaning.''

---

[53]*The Shape of the Church To Come* (New York: Seabury, 1974) 54.

Chapter 3
LIBERAL MISUNDERSTANDING OF THE INTERACTION BETWEEN BIBLICAL CRITICISM AND DOGMA

The preceding chapter studied how the church has moved from what was written about divine revelation in the NT to what was proclaimed dogmatically at a later period. There are scholars on either end of the Catholic spectrum who are unwilling to tolerate the kinds of trajectory I have posited in that chapter. On the conservative extreme of the spectrum there is an attempt to read the NT so that the later dogmas were already known in NT times. I shall deal with that in Chapter 4 below, but in this chapter let me concern myself with an example of the liberal extreme of the Catholic spectrum which interprets the NT so radically that it becomes virtually contradictory to later dogma. First, I shall illustrate some nuances of NT exegesis as a caution against too easily assuming a radical stance. Then, I shall concentrate on the claims of a scholar who has attracted attention with his assumptions about the direction of Catholic historical-critical exegesis, namely, Thomas Sheehan.

ILLUSTRATIONS OF NUANCE IN NT EXEGESIS

Most Catholic NT scholars (as well as Protestants) could agree that the Gospels are remarkably vague as to whether Jesus explicitly claimed to be the Messiah. In the first three Gospels where one evangelist reports an affirmative answer by Jesus to the question of messiahship, almost inevitably another evangelist has a vague answer. A careful study of the way in which titles are used for Jesus in the various strata of the NT has led to the conclusion that Jesus tended to reveal his self-identity indirectly during his lifetime, in part because expectations about the role he might be fulfilling did not agree with his own understanding of his role. Yet Christians in the post-resurrectional period were intensely concerned about making explicit Jesus' identity, because confession of "the name of Jesus" was part of baptismal entry into the church. In order to explicate their christology (i.e., their evaluation of Jesus), they reunderstood the traditional terminology they adopted from Judaism, shaping it to fit Jesus. The tremendous reality of who Jesus was led to an adaptation of all existing theological language. Therefore, they could enthusiastically discern that Jesus was the Messiah, but for them Messiah had less political connotations than it had in much of Judaism (and probably had on the lips of Jesus' interrogators).

Most Scripture scholars would see nothing destructive in such an approach. It does not deny that Jesus was aware of his identity; rather it affirms simply that he may not have found a traditional term an adequate description of that identity.[54] This approach does not deny that Christians were correct in affirming that Jesus was the Messiah; but it recognizes that Christians grew in an appreciation of Jesus and had to reinterpret traditional language to suit his greatness. How astonishing, then, to find both intelligent ultraconservatives and intelligent liberals claiming that most NT scholars deny that Jesus was the Messiah or that he knew who he was. They even have "Catholic biblical scholars" *en masse* affirming that the early Christians reshaped Jesus drastically, distorting the authentic Jesus. The ultraconservatives will use such a claim to show the extent to which biblical scholars (whom they consider extreme radicals) have done away with the essentials of Christianity. The liberals will use such a claim as a scholarly backing for their own complete freedom to interpret Jesus in modern categories. In making such claims, too often both extremists lump Catholic NT scholars with some systematic theologians who might well supply evidence for their claims.

Another example: NT scholars have had to deal with the complexity of church development that emerges when the individual works of the NT are arranged chronologically and studied without transposing data

---

[54]See *Jesus* (footnote 47 above) 79ff., and my article, "Did Jesus Know He Was God?", *BTB* 15 (April 1985) 74–79.

from one document to another written independently. Let me list almost telegraphically some of the indisputable *results* that emerge:[55] the term "church" appears on Jesus' lips only in Matthew's Gospel; there are no clear directives from him on church organization in any Gospel; the only reason Jesus himself gives for choosing the Twelve is that they may sit on twelve thrones judging the twelve tribes of Israel; the term "apostle" is applied to others than the Twelve in the NT; no evidence can be found that all those called apostles founded church communities in a missionary enterprise—indeed, there is little evidence in the NT that most of the Twelve Apostles founded churches; figures called "bishops" appear in *some* NT churches; these "bishops" seem to be a plural group in a church, wholly or partially interchangeable with "presbyters"; there is no clear NT instance of a bishop singled out from the presbyters as the sole highest authority in a church (although in Jerusalem, without the title, James has a precedence over the elders, perhaps because of his status as a relative of Jesus, the Davidic king); when the pattern of one bishop outranking presbyters and presiding over a church does emerge clearly in the writings of Ignatius of Antioch (*ca.* A.D. 110), it seems to be a recent step, and indeed a step not yet in place in a church like Rome; even in Ignatius, no information is given on how a contemporary bishop gets his office; a Christian document of the same period, the *Didache,* shows a situation where the readers are urged to appoint for themselves bishops and deacons, who will substitute for the current, rather hectic dependence upon apostles and prophets, many of whom are itinerant.

Granting such confusing and partial evidence, scholars suspect that, while in some instances (e.g., some of the Pauline churches) the pattern of a church directed by a group of bishops may have developed in an apostle's lifetime and, indeed, some bishops may have been chosen by an apostle, in most cases bishops (or more precisely presbyter-bishops) were a post-apostolic development. The pattern of one bishop over the presbyters was an even later first-century development in some churches and became widespread-to-universal only in the second century. The large block of centrist Catholic NT scholars would not contend that this development negates the church doctrine reiterated at Vatican II that bishops are the successors of the apostles. Yet the scholars would insist

---

[55]The evidence is given in detail in *PB* (throughout) and in *CMB* 96–106, 124–46.

that the biblical evidence carefully evaluated does nuance the doctrine.[56] Even if it was only after two centuries that the one-bishop-per-church pattern had emerged universally, with the bishop having ultimate responsibility for administration and sanctification, still the pastoral authority and care exercised by apostles (a wider group than the Twelve) eventually did pass to the bishops. What modern Catholic NT scholars are challenging is a historically unsubstantiated understanding of apostolic succession as if the Twelve Apostles who were appointed by Jesus in turn appointed in each church a single bishop on whom hands were laid as a successor. No one can prove that. (Even the early writer, Clement of Rome, who gives a simplified picture of apostolic succession, betrays no knowledge of the practice of having only one bishop in each church.)

It is puzzling, then, why intelligent people at each end of the Catholic spectrum, conservative and liberal, state sweepingly that biblical scholars deny apostolic succession. Apparently, both ends of the spectrum insist on a naive and almost tactile understanding of apostolic succession in a one-to-one line. For ultraconservatives the distorted charge that "biblical scholars deny apostolic succession" is a proof that these scholars are undermining fundamental church constitution. For liberals the distorted contention that "biblical scholars deny that the bishops are the successors of the apostles" is proof that the bishopric can be dispensed with and we are free to return to a pristine egalitarianism in the church—most of the time to an egalitarianism that, in fact, is scarcely demonstrable by critical scholarship even in those periods or places in the NT picture in which bishops had not yet developed!

I could go on giving example after example; for in no case (the virginal conception, the bodily resurrection, the sacraments, Mary, etc.) do I think that centrist Catholic NT scholarship denies Catholic doctrine understood in its complex historical development, even though conservatives and liberals both freely attribute such denials. Lest, however, the discussion become too general, let me concentrate on an intelligent writer from the liberal end of the spectrum who illustrates the contentions I have just been making.

---

[56]I made this point in *PB* 73; see footnote 50 above for the ultraconservative reaction to "nuance."

THOMAS SHEEHAN'S LIBERAL CONSENSUS

A professor of philosophy at Loyola University (Chicago), Thomas Sheehan wrote a review of Hans Küng's *Eternal Life?* in the June 14, 1984 *New York Review of Books.* The review was entitled "Revolution in the Church," a not inappropriate title for his analysis of a "liberal consensus" among Roman Catholics today that is undermining the classic presentation of church doctrine. *Commonweal* magazine later (Aug. 10, Sept. 21, Oct. 5, 1984) reported the responses of many Catholic scholars to Sheehan's review, but perhaps the most telling summary was *Commonweal*'s own estimate of Sheehan as a post-Christian agnostic.

By "liberal consensus" Sheehan states that he means "the scientific methods employed and the conclusions generated by Catholic exegetes and theologians internationally recognized in their fields." As his prime examples of such scholars he lists twelve (R. Schnackenburg, R. E. Brown, R. Murphy, P. Benoit, J. P. Meier, J. A. Fitzmyer, D. M. Stanley, R. Pesch, W. Kasper, D. Tracy, E. Schillebeeckx, H. Küng) of which the first eight are Scripture exegetes and the last four are theologians. Sheehan does not acknowledge the incongruity of his listing—he has joined six scholars who have been appointed by popes to Roman commissions (Brown, Benoit, Fitzmyer, and Stanley to the Pontifical Biblical Commission and Schnackenburg and Kasper to the Pontifical Theological Commission) with two scholars toward whom Rome has been exceedingly negative (Küng has been deprived of the right to teach in a Catholic theological chair, Schillebeeckx brought to Rome and corrected for his theological conclusions about ministry). Is it really plausible that a consensus exists between those scholars whom Rome has specifically honored and those of whom it has specifically disapproved?

The consensus becomes even more dubious when one remembers that among the very critical reviewers of works by Küng and Schillebeeckx have been some whom Sheehan joins in this consensus. Certainly I for one have expressed my disagreement with both the methods and the conclusions of the two scholars, and Kasper has been a strong critic of Küng. (Of course, this criticism was done within the proper bounds of scholarly dispute, respectfully and without the slightest intention of questioning orthodoxy—a questioning that, in my judgment, belongs to the magisterium alone even if ultraconservatives think they have this right.) Sheehan acknowledges in passing that the members of his consensus do not necessarily agree with each other, but he does not seem to realize that the extent of the disagreement means that most of those he names would feel *exceedingly uncomfortable and out of place* in the "liberal consensus" that he has constructed. Certainly, most of them would reject firmly the christology and ecclesiology that Sheehan describes as emerging from the consensus!

Later on, when Sheehan cites books to footnote his conclusions, he confuses the situation further by adding (without indication) Protestant authors to what is supposedly a liberal Catholic consensus. In reference to the resurrection, for instance, he makes a hodgepodge presentation involving Küng and Schillebeeckx (who are weak or ambiguous on the bodily resurrection), Fuller and Wilckens (Protestants), McBrien and me. I doubt that any reader could guess that I (and probably most of the other eight Catholic Scripture exegetes Sheehan listed in his beginning rostrum of consensus scholars) would drastically qualify and even reject much of the consensus view of the resurrection that he presents. For instance, I could agree that the first "literary appearance" of the *story* of the empty tomb is in the Gospel of Mark, forty years after the event; but I have written explicitly that the *fact* of the empty tomb was in my judgment part of Christian understanding from the beginning,[57] since Christian preaching of the resurrection would have been refuted from the start if the enemies of Jesus could have pointed to his body in the tomb. Sheehan cites Küng and Schillebeeckx for the idea that Christian faith in the risen Jesus came from his appearances independently of the empty tomb. That is probably so; but unlike Küng and Schillebeeckx, I have written that the emptiness of the tomb gave an essential coloring to the preaching about the risen Jesus—"being raised" implied *bodily* resurrection; the one who appeared had a risen *body* that was no longer in the tomb (p. 38 above). That is quite unlike Sheehan's indications of the directions of resurrection scholarship (which are mostly the directions of Küng).

Also seemingly citing Küng, but in no way distinguishing his view from the views of the supposed liberal consensus, Sheehan portrays a Jesus who "saw himself not as God or the Messiah, but as a Jewish

---

[57]See footnote 28 above; also my comments in the Symposium on P. Perkins' *Resurrection* in *Horizons* 12 (#2, Fall 1985).

prophet''—a view that, as I explained above, is a negative exaggeration of what most Catholic exegetes hold about the implicit christology of Jesus' ministry.

Granting what I have written earlier in this article, the reader probably does not need much guidance to see how I would react against Sheehan's presentation of liberal consensus ecclesiology: "And it seems he [Jesus] did not know he was supposed to establish the Holy Roman Catholic and Apostolic Church with St. Peter as the first in a long line of infallible popes." From studying the NT evidence presupposed but not explained by Sheehan, I would say that in his lifetime Jesus called around him a community of disciples as a renewed Israel. Fortified by Jesus' victory over death in the resurrection, and by the gift of the Spirit, these disciples, in imitation of Jesus' own baptism, made the formal step of requiring a visible sign for adherents to Jesus. The community, which now began to be more and more a group distinct within Judaism, soon adopted the term "church" (the Semitic equivalent of which had described Israel in the desert and so might not have been foreign to Jesus' thought patterns). Very old references to this "church" indicate not only the primary place of apostles (some of them the Twelve to whom Jesus had given priority in the renewal of Israel) but also the idea that the gospel would attract people from East and West and give the community a catholicity. When understood with nuance, then, the proposition that Jesus Christ founded the one, holy, catholic, and apostolic church is not necessarily foreign to modern exegesis of the NT.[58] Sheehan's negative description quoted above presupposes an oversimplified understanding of church foundation, involving *explicit* intention on Jesus' part during his ministry—an explicitness not necessarily a part of Catholic doctrine on the subject. As for the rest of what I quoted from Sheehan, the ecumenical book *Peter in the New Testament* (Paulist/Augsburg 1973), done by Protestant and Catholic exegetes together, would give a nuanced appreciation of the major role of Peter in the NT times, even as the official

---

[58]The very perceptive article by F. S. Fiorenza, "Seminar on Rahner's Ecclesiology: Jesus and the Foundation of the Church," *PCTSA* 33 (1975) 229–54, critiques Küng's statement that Jesus is *not* what is generally understood as a founder of a church. He points out that, while Küng has a more critical control of the NT data, Rahner has better theological perception in upholding the traditional conviction that Jesus founded a church.

Lutheran/Roman Catholic Dialogue in the USA gave a nuanced evaluation of Catholic dogmas on the papacy—an outlook far more positive than Sheehan's derogatory statement about Peter as the first in a line of infallible popes.[59]

It may be that Sheehan knows much of what I report; but his tendency in the review of Küng to set up straw men easily knocked down is not likely to enlighten readers as to the true state of Catholic NT exegesis which is centrist rather than liberal, and is not destructive of Catholic dogma. Systematic theologians can speak for themselves, but I suspect that most of them would react just as strongly as does this biblical scholar in questioning Sheehan's notion of a liberal consensus and in demanding more nuance about christology and ecclesiology.

As a final reference to Sheehan, and as a theme that will lead into the discussion of the next chapter, let me quote his "liberal consensus" presentation of the virginal conception in modern exegesis: "Nor did Jesus know that his mother, Mary, had remained a virgin in the very act of conceiving him. . . . Most likely Mary told Jesus what she herself knew of his origins: that he had a natural father and was born not in Bethlehem but in Nazareth." To footnote much of this, he cites my books *VCBRJ* and *BM*, quoting my views thus: " 'The totality of the *scientifically* controllable evidence leaves an unresolved problem' which calls for ecumenical discussion and, ultimately, resolution within the frame of the teaching authority of the Church." The single quotation marks in what I have just cited are my own words; and I give Sheehan credit that at least he indicated that I appealed to the teaching authority of the Church. What he did not mention are my judgments that the scientifically controllable evidence *favors* the historicity of the virginal conception, and that the Church teaches infallibly that Mary conceived as a virgin.[60] I have indicated no support whatsoever for the suggestion that Jesus did not know that his mother had remained a virgin in the act of conception, and that Mary told Jesus that he had a natural father.

I recognize that some of Küng's remarks seem to dispense with the virginal conception, as do a few Catholic biblical scholars (footnote 24 above). But the majority of Catholic exegetes who have written on the

---

[59] I have expressed my own views in *BRCFC* 63–83.
[60] See footnotes 11 and 26 above.

subject do not handle the material so radically; and in the ecumenical book *MNT* (291–92) Protestant and Catholic scholars came closer to my cautious conclusion than to Sheehan's supposed liberal consensus.

WHY AND WITH WHAT RESULTS?

I selected Sheehan as an example of how an intelligent represent-ative of the liberal end of the Catholic spectrum could misunderstand and misrepresent the centrist thrust of Catholic biblical exegesis. Let me now ask briefly two questions: why and with what results? In answering the first of these two questions many of my remarks are equally applicable to a misunderstanding of Catholic biblical exegesis on the ultraconserv-ative end of the spectrum.

Why? I am not a profound psychological analyst: but it seems to me that both liberals and conservatives falsify what biblical scholars write by fitting it into preconceptions derived from elsewhere. Both recognize the surface novelty of Catholic NT exegesis, but not its depth novelty. The *surface novelty* is that the old ways of looking at biblical issues have changed: we cannot assume that eyewitnesses of Jesus' ministry wrote the Gospels; what the evangelists wrote about Jesus in the last third of the first century goes considerably beyond the perception of Jesus in the first third of the century; not every detail narrated in the Gospels is to be taken literally; one cannot attribute later dogmas to the explicit words or consciousness of Jesus in Galilee; one must think in terms of "Jesus Christ," i.e., the Jesus of the ministry understood in the light of post-resurrectional faith in his full reality as the Christ. For Catholic extrem-ists of either type this seems a recrudescence of the rationalism or mod-ernism of times past which drove a wedge between the Jesus of history and the Christ of faith, with the result that Christian doctrine is deprived of historical foundations. They do not recognize the *deeper novelty* that contemporary Catholic NT exegesis (and much contemporary Protestant exegesis as well) is much more careful about continuity between the pre-resurrectional and the post-resurrectional. Certainly there is a new di-mension after the resurrection; but many of us think of it as a recognition of the reality that was already there, a making explicit of what was im-plicit, and a trajectory or line of development in a direction already be-gun in the ministry. Thus, in a concept of the Gospels as representing developing tradition, the issue is not one of creation from nothing, or of symbolism without basis, or of falsification; but rather one of the gradual penetration of how "God was in Christ reconciling the world to Himself" (II Cor 5:19)—a penetration that, although guided by the Spirit as we know from our faith, followed ordinary human rules of vocabulary development and growth through encounter with new questions. This insistence on continuity in development, which distinguishes the centrist approach to the NT from an older rationalism, makes it plausible to see a bridge between the NT critically considered and the dogmas of the subsequent church catholic.

Ultraconservatives, stunned by the new historical observations of critical exegesis, interpret that exegesis as a rejection of church dogmas precisely because they identify the dogmas with the literalist scriptural underpinning that was previously inculcated in Roman Catholic circles. Ultraliberals also attempt to fit modern critical exegesis into a presculptured mold. Often liberal ideas have been shaped by theologians whose primary source of reflection is not exegesis but philosophy or sociology, or by theologians who have consciously or unconsciously chosen a radical, rather than a centrist, exegesis. My personal criticism of both Küng and Schillebeeckx, for instance, is that they have read biblical studies with a bias favoring the most radical conclusions. Because modern Catholic theologians and exegetes are both engaged in a process of rethinking the implications of Scripture and dogma for the 20th century (an age of historical sophistication), it is sometimes supposed their work is all harmonious. Greater attention has to be paid to differences among them,[61] and weight has to be given to the fact that both centrist exegetes and centrist theologians disclaim radical statements. A real consensus would not be ultraconservative; neither would it be liberal or radical.

With what result? The results of Sheehan's article are diverse. The reaction of some interested Catholic nonprofessionals who spoke to me about it was saddening. Not having the expertise to recognize its exaggerations, they wondered were our best and most intelligent scholars off on such radical departures from tradition. In other words, they felt caught between what seemed to be the horrendous "liberal consensus"

---

[61]The joining of the names of Küng and Schillebeeckx (who have had difficulties with the Roman Doctrinal Congregation) to the names of centrist Catholic biblical exegetes is not peculiar to Sheehan; it is a favorite ploy of the ultraconservatives, hoping to create the impression that all modern biblical and theological thought is frowned on by Rome.

and a return to an indefensible and suffocating conservatism. Part of my reason for writing this chapter was to offer reassurance that there remains the option of a centrist position to which, in fact, most scholars (including those whom Sheehan wrongly puts in his liberal consensus) still adhere.

The ultraconservative Catholic press has given Sheehan a great deal of attention—one is surprised to find that the scathing pamphleteers of the Right even know of the *New York Review of Books!* Triumphantly, they proclaim that this liberal writer of impeccable credentials proves they were correct in arguing that the best known Catholic scholars are all extreme radicals drifting away from the church. In making this claim one pundit (James Hitchcock in the *National Catholic Register*) went out on a limb to predict that the members of the "liberal consensus" would not protest Sheehan's article because they knew that it was a correct analysis. How bad a prophecy! There was immediate and vociferous protest by those incorrectly classified as liberals, pointing out misrepresentation.[62]

The thrust of the ultraconservative use of the Sheehan article has now shifted. True, it is argued, the scholars have responded to Sheehan, but their response shows how liberal they are (*Fellowship of Catholic Scholars Newsletter,* Nov. 1984). After all, they did not disown historical critical exegesis. (Why should they disown it, since their use of critical exegesis follows directives from Rome itself?) They did not refer to the magisterium of the church in their answers. (Some of them did; but in any case, is not the very reason for disclaiming Sheehan's thesis the loyalty of the respondees to the magisterium, and have not over half of Sheehan's "liberal consensus" been honored by the magisterium through papal appointment to Roman commissions?) They did not deny that the "liberal consensus" dominates Catholic higher education. (Since Sheehan's liberal consensus is a fictional mingling of centrist scholars with a few others who might be considered liberal, an accurate description is that *centrist* exegesis and theological teaching dominate Catholic education, and that is all to the good.)

If I may leave myself out of the picture, the fact that students in

---

[62]Besides the *Commonweal* articles cited at the beginning of my treatment of Sheehan, note G. O'Collins, *The Tablet* (Oct. 13,20, 1984); J. A. Fitzmyer and R. E. Brown, "Danger Also from the Left," *TBT* 23 (#2; March 1985) 105–10.

theology read the biblical works of R. Schnackenburg, R. Murphy, P. Benoit, J. P. Meier, and J. A. Fitzmyer—to cite those named by Sheehan—is the best protection that the misrepresentation of Catholic exegesis as liberal or radical promoted both by Sheehan (and, of course, by the scions of the Catholic ultraconservative press) will be recognized and rejected. It also offers the best hope that in the future more Catholics will be able to make distinctions that will enable them to see the extent to which modern Catholic critical exegesis supports a properly nuanced understanding of church dogmas.

Chapter 4
CONSERVATIVE MISUNDERSTANDING OF
THE INTERACTION BETWEEN
BIBLICAL CRITICISM AND DOGMA

L et me turn now to the other end of the spectrum and the conservative
or ultraconservative attempt to avoid the trajectories of doctrinal development I described in Chapter 2—an attempt centered on finding
more in the NT than most critical exegetes can find. As examples of this
attempt I shall comment upon two scholars, John McHugh (a non-po-
lemic NT exegete) and René Laurentin (a polemic mariologist). Since
both of them have concentrated on the infancy narratives, let me preface
my response to their works with remarks about the rationale behind the
infancy narrative debate.

SPECIAL DIFFICULTIES ABOUT INFANCY NARRATIVE
HISTORY

There are rationalists who, under the rubric of historical criticism,
deny factuality to all the miracles of Jesus, attributing to him a no-more-
than-human status. In this book I have resisted wasting time on extreme
positions, and I consider such antimiraculous rationalism an extreme.
How does a centrist historical criticism consider the infancy narratives?
As explained in Chapter 1 (pp. 12-14 above) centrist Roman Catholic
exegetes, following the lead of the Pontifical Biblical Commission, rec-

ognize a development from Jesus to the Gospel accounts of the ministry, but insist that the line of development began with historical memories of Jesus' deeds and words. Such centrist exegesis involves no necessary rejection of miracles or of the supernatural in the public career of Jesus. Yet for four principal reasons many centrist exegetes find special problems in dealing with the historicity of the Matthean and Lucan narratives of Jesus' conception, birth and infancy. These reasons are:

(1) One does not know where the information about Jesus' birth came from. For the public ministry of Jesus from his baptism on, apostolic witnesses, including members of the Twelve, are named in the NT. But neither Luke nor Matthew tells us whence he got his information about Jesus' birth. Of the two family figures who would know best what happened, Joseph never appears during Jesus' public ministry (probably being dead by that time), and Mary is mentioned for the last time as being with other believers *before* Pentecost. (The idea that Mary lived on for a long while among the Jerusalem Christians and ultimately supplied the infancy information recorded in Luke or in Matthew is pure speculation, not based on either the NT or very early Christian tradition.) Biblical critics are being honest, not skeptical, when they point to a lack of knowledge on the source of infancy information.

(2) Most of the information given in the two infancy narratives is not confirmed elsewhere in the NT. Nowhere else do we find an independent NT indication that Jesus was born at Bethlehem (Matt, Luke), that his birth caused a furor throughout all Jerusalem (Matt), that a star came to rest over Bethlehem (Matt), that Herod slaughtered children while seeking to kill Jesus (Matt), that Jesus and John the Baptist were relatives (Luke), or that Jesus was virginally conceived (Matt, Luke). As I have already mentioned, on the last point there have been attempts to find the virginal conception in Paul's reference to Jesus born of a woman (Gal 4:4), in Mark's reference to Jesus as son of Mary (Mark 6:3), or in John's reference to becoming a child of God (John 1:13 read as singular). However, few scholars support the virginal-conception interpretation of these verses, and those who claim to find it should warn readers of the adventuresome character of their claims. If one did not have the infancy narratives, one would never think of a virginal conception from these other verses.

(3) Some of the events narrated in the infancy narratives were in the public domain and could have left some record in the histories of the

period. No such record is found. In Josephus' detailed listing of the horrors wrought by Herod the Great there is never a reference to his slaughtering children at Bethlehem. Neither Roman nor Jewish records mention a Roman census of Galilee during the reign of Herod the Great, nor a worldwide census under Augustus, nor a governorship over Syria by Quirinius as early as the reign of Herod the Great—all of which are affirmed explicitly or implicitly by Luke. There is no record of a star such as Matthew describes. Again, there have been strained attempts to confirm any or all of the above from historical or astronomical records, but none has proved convincing to the large body of scholars. The argument that these things are not implausible does not suffice when one argues for historicity. For instance, the ancients believed that signs in the heavens often accompanied the births of great men or women. That means that Matthew's story of the star announcing the birth of "the King of the Jews" would have sounded plausible to an ancient audience. But a writer of fiction or a popular storyteller would want to sound plausible and, indeed, might write a story of greater popular plausibility than one produced by an author limited to fact. We recognize this through the saying, "Truth is stranger than fiction."

(4) The two birth stories do not agree with each other. Matthew would lead the reader to assume that Joseph and Mary lived at Bethlehem where they had a house (2:11), for he takes great pains to explain why they left Bethlehem to go to settle in Nazareth (2:22–23). His account leaves no logical space for a census that brought them temporarily to Bethlehem from Nazareth, such as Luke describes. Luke reports nothing about magi, a star, and the flight to Egypt; nor does his account of a peaceful return to Nazareth through Jerusalem leave room for such events. These discrepancies make it extremely dubious that *both* accounts could have come from a family source or that both accounts are historical. The contention that Luke's account at least is historical runs up against the non-verifiability of the census and the fact that Luke describes inaccurately the process of purification/presentation (despite forced attempts to explain away "their purification" in Luke 2:22— only Mary needed purification).

In evaluating the above, I would insist that the four difficulties do *not* prove that the infancy narratives are not historical. That is why I have consistently resisted statements such as: "There were no magi"; "There was no star."[63] But the four difficulties make it clear that doubts about the historicity of the infancy narratives need not flow from rationalism or skepticism but simply from weighing the evidence. THE BURDEN OF PROOF LIES ON THOSE WHO AFFIRM HISTORICITY, since it is not clear that either evangelist intended a historical account or was in a position to give one. One cannot avoid this issue by facilely speaking of inspiration, for as I insisted above (p. 12), inspiration does not tell us what type of literature we are dealing with: the infancy narratives might be inspired history or they might be inspired popular imaginative accounts, or some other less-than-history genre. Nor can one resort to the principle that in the Bible one presupposes history unless there is evidence to the contrary. A recent papal statement (footnote 5 above) insists that the Bible is a library, and in a library one has no right to make an assumption about the nature of a book until one has investigated that book.

Let me now turn to two conservative scholars with whom I have differences over the infancy narratives, differences that reflect their stance on the relationship of Bible to dogma.

JOHN MCHUGH

In 1975 Father John McHugh wrote *The Mother of Jesus in the New Testament* (Garden City, NY: Doubleday), a volume of over 500 pages. Facing a Protestant-versus-Catholic impasse over Marian doctrines such as the Immaculate Conception and the Assumption, McHugh (p. xxvii) sought to show that these doctrines "are either plainly expressed or necessarily implied in holy Scripture"—a position that would meet the Protestant insistence on *sola Scriptura* ("Scripture alone"). I wrote a review of the book in the October 25, 1975 *America* (pp. 260–63) arguing that McHugh's solution is both unnecessary and impossible. My principle, which I have now explained at length in Chapter 2 above, is that while all dogma must be expressed or implied in the revelation that is Jesus Christ, all dogma does not have to be expressed or implied in the NT (which attests a first-century understanding of the revelation).

I recognized that McHugh's exegesis was intelligent, mildly criti-

---

[63]*BM* 189, n. 28.

cal, and not fundamentalist; but I found that he bypassed the tough problems of modern exegesis. He argued that Paul must have known of the virginal conception since he traveled with Luke, without reporting that many modern exegetes doubt that the author of Luke-Acts was the traveling companion of Paul. He spent over 50 pages listing arguments and patristic guesses about the identity of those called "the brothers" of Jesus in the NT (pp. 40-43 above), without asking sufficiently whether these ancient patristic writers were in any position to know facts about Jesus' family or were simply making pious guesses by continuing stories that they thought to be true. He harmonized disparate material in the Gospels, assuming that John was the "beloved disciple" of the Fourth Gospel, that Mary lived with John after the crucifixion and told John about Jesus' infancy narrative, and that Luke drew his infancy material from such a Johannine intermediary. I judge such a theory untenable; for there is no infancy information in the Fourth Gospel, and Luke's contention that John the Baptist was a relative of Jesus runs directly against the statement in John 1:31 that the Baptist had no previous knowledge of Jesus. McHugh explained the sword that will pierce Mary's soul (Luke 2:35) in terms of Mary's standing at the foot of the cross—a scene that Luke never narrates and may not have known, since he does not mention Mary among the women at the crucifixion. McHugh treated scarcely at all what may be the oldest scene in Christian writing involving Mary, the scene in Mark 3:31–35 where Jesus proclaims his family to be, not the mother and brothers who have come looking for him, but his disciples who do the will of God—a scene difficult for mariology (see pp. 89-90 below).

In 1977 I published my study of the infancy narratives (*BM*) and in 1978 there appeared *MNT*, an ecumenical study of Mary of which I was an editor. John McHugh wrote a review of these two works in *The Ampleforth Review* (1980) 43–57. It was a gentlemanly, scholarly review that had good possibilities for intelligent discussion. The editors asked me to give a brief response, and I did so in the same issue on pages 57–60. Let me mention some of the points of disagreement, again expressing my gratitude, as I did there, for the care and unfailing courtesy of Father McHugh. It is a relief to see a Catholic scholar who can dissent from a historical-critical book on the infancy narratives without resorting to polemical attack. Let me list points numerically:

(1) McHugh notes several places in *BM* where I differ "signifi-

cantly from other Catholic writers'' in my exegesis. If one notices the footnotes in which he lists these writers with whom I disagree, they are mostly French Catholics (Laurentin, Léon-Dufour, Lyonnet, Cazelles, Benoit) who wrote on infancy material in the 1950s and 60s. I have criticized McHugh's own book on Mary for being overly influenced by such thought. There are many German and American Catholic writers on the infancy narratives who have also disagreed with French tendencies (Schnackenburg, Schürmann, Vögtle, Bourke, and Fitzmyer, to name a few, and I would add the more recent French writer, Lucien Legrand). Thus in self-evaluation I deem it more accurate to say I disagree *with one group* of Catholic writers and agree with another. The ecumenical book *MNT* shows that I am far from unrepresentative of church-concerned NT exegetes of all faiths.

(2) McHugh states that, on the basis of a historical-critical approach, both *BM* and *MNT* assert, ''The historicity of the virginal conception must remain an open question, as must the issue of Mary's lifelong virginity.'' Although I do not wish to get embroiled in terminological debate, it is no accident that on the pages of the two books that he gives as references for his statement one will not find the expression ''open question.'' In my earlier book, *VCBRJ*, I stated on p. 25: ''It is probably inaccurate to describe the problem of the virginal conception as an open question for Catholics.'' Of course, McHugh is correct in that both *BM* and *MNT* say that the historical-critical method of interpretation does not offer adequate evidence to solve the historicity of either the virginal conception or the perpetual virginity of Mary; but both books point to church teaching as a possible way of resolving these issues and of going beyond the impasse left by the limitations of the historical-critical method.[64] I hope that I am not simply playing with words when I insist that the two Marian issues would have to ''*remain* open questions'' only for those who pretend that the historical-critical method is all-sufficient. Catholics are not in that position and neither are many Protestants.

(3) As I mentioned above (p. 42), the rather dubious *Protevangelium of James* purports to be early family tradition indicating that Mary remained a virgin after the birth of Jesus. Reflection on the role of Mary in God's plan of salvation through the guidance of the Holy Spirit grad-

---

[64]See *VCBRJ* 66, note 117 with a reference back to p. 35; *BM* 529, note 29; *MNT* 292.

ually led the church to insist that the continued virginity of Mary (however it received that idea) is an essential understanding of her role in the plan of salvation. Does a knowledge of the truth taught by the church change one's reading of the NT evidence? Negatively, it prevents one from reading the ambiguous passages on the subject to mean that Mary did *not* remain a virgin. But it does not make the *literal sense* of any text pertaining to the issue one bit more favorable to the virginity of Mary than it is without church insight. And this is so for the simple reason that nothing in our faith requires us to hold that the NT authors knew that Mary remained a virgin. It is a wrong understanding of inerrancy to think that first-century writers had to have solutions to issues that had not been raised and were not of theological significance in their time. When McHugh talks about the role of church doctrine in exegesis, I am afraid that some will interpret this to mean that the church can settle many historical issues for which it has no special charism and no extraordinary guidance of the Holy Spirit, or that the church's charism changes evidence. To decide what an individual NT author thought about Mary's perpetual virginity the church needs the aid of scholarship, a frail aid to be sure, but one through which the Holy Spirit also works. I do not look to the church to settle the issue of what an individual NT author meant (and in fact I think it has never done so). That is why I wrote in *BM* (p. 9): "I see no reason why a Catholic's understanding of what Matthew and Luke meant in their infancy narratives should be different from a Protestant's." I look to the church to tell me what a NT passage has eventually come to mean for my belief. I also look to the church to help resolve the doctrinal import of ambiguous NT evidence, and I think it has done this in the question of the perpetual virginity of Mary.

(4) McHugh obviously feels that the limited results of the historical-critical method may scandalize, frighten, or discourage Catholic students; and in presenting the Bible he wants to insist more strongly on church guidance *in exegesis*. But in dealing with Catholic students I have the opposite fear. Because of Reformation struggles they have been indoctrinated with later church teaching and *en masse* had never read attentively what is in the Scriptures except through the glasses of that later teaching. How can we be afraid of too much historical-critical exegesis in the church when there has hardly been any at all? I think it extremely important to lay out before Catholic readers the bare bones of the evidence. The skeleton is never an adequate picture of a total human body,

but one will never understand the body unless one has seen the skeleton. A frank confrontation with the kind of evidence uncovered by an intelligent use of the historical-critical method can bring Catholic students to appreciate the need for a teaching church, as I demonstrated above in Chapter 2. Is it so destructive if Catholics find that historical investigation of the evidence does not prove (or disprove) the virginal conception of Jesus or the perpetual virginity of Mary and that these doctrines must be believed on the authority of a teaching church? This is far healthier than pretending, as some would have us do, that our status as Catholics enables us to find more historical information or evidence in the literal sense of the text than can our Protestant brothers and sisters. That mentality must lead us to look on those who disagree with us as fools or knaves rather than as people who do not accept the same degree of church authority we accept.

(5) On his last page McHugh says that the two books, *BM* and *MNT*, show what can be known about the biblical text as *words of men*, but he suggests that we need a methodology that shows what the text means as a *verbum Dei*, ''word of God.'' I firmly reject this type of distinction. The word of God is expressed in the Bible *in* the words of men who lived at a particular time and had only a partial glimpse of the truth (as do human beings at any time, including our own). The methodology used in these two books shows us God's plan of salvation in regard to Jesus' birth and in regard to Mary as it was known and portrayed by people of the first century. It is bad methodologically to read back later insights into their words found in the NT—just as it is a dangerous lack of subtlety not to see a connection between their understanding and later insights. The most crucial difference between McHugh and me may lie in a judgment on whether God's revelation, given to us once and for all in Jesus Christ, had to be understood totally by first-century Christians. I think that it did not and that those Christians wrote the NT with only a partial understanding of the revelation they described. That is why I maintain the need for a church which through the Holy Spirit can enable later generations to see in Christ aspects that first Christians did not see when they wrote their text. This hindsight may make NT texts more meaningful to us; it does not change what the original authors intended. The goal of these two books, *BM* and *MNT*, was to discover not simply what the authors meant as human beings, but what they meant as human beings who were guided by the Spirit to speak *God's word with limited*

insight. In closing my remarks on McHugh, let me pay him the compliment that his earnest and polite questioning led to my writing Chapter 2 of this book. That chapter is the kernel of my response to him.

RENÉ LAURENTIN

A French mariologist, Fr. Laurentin has recently completed an enthusiastic work on the more than 900 appearances of Mary in Jugoslavia since 1981—appearances discounted by the local bishop and treated with extreme circumspection by the Vatican. Early in his mariological career, Laurentin wrote a book on the structure and theology of the Lucan infancy narrative.[65] Composed in the atmosphere of a precritical period of Catholic NT exegesis, the book made an important contribution since it was not primarily concerned with NT historical criticism but with OT symbolic background employed by Luke. Although Catholic scholars did not accept all the OT symbols that Laurentin proposed for Luke's presentation of Mary (in particular, Mary as the Ark of the Covenant was challenged), most recognized that much of the symbolic background was valid. If anything, Laurentin's stress on OT background moved Catholic exegesis away from a fascination with historical issues in the Lucan infancy narrative.

A decade later Laurentin wrote another book on the Lucan infancy narrative, concentrating on the discovery of the child Jesus in the Temple.[66] This was much less satisfactory; for it crossed from symbolism into history, making it apparent that Laurentin thought the scene to be so historical that he could reconstruct Mary's psychological reaction at the moment of finding the child. In *BM* (pp. 491, 484) I expressed politely my disagreement with Laurentin's foray into history. I noted in particular Laurentin's recalling a Roman discussion that if one were to deny that Mary knew Jesus' divinity from the annunciation on, one would not be "sufficiently generous to the Madonna." I stated the following: "While I am a Roman Catholic and share with Laurentin an acceptance of Church dogma on Mary, I reject resolutely his using in an exegetical and historical study the principle: 'One cannot suppose that

---

[65]*Structure et Théologie de Luc I-II* (Paris: Gabalda, 1957).

[66]*Jésus au Temple: Mystère de Pâques et foi de Marie en Luc 2,48–50* (Paris: Gabalda, 1966).

Mary lacked the knowledge that befits the Mother of God.' From the Christian acceptance of Mary as the Mother of God, one may learn of her sanctity, but not the historicity of her growth in knowledge.''

My subject of concern in this chapter, however, is Laurentin's book on the infancy narratives which appeared in French in 1982 and in English in 1985.[67] I have written a long review of the French in *Marianum* 47 (1985) 15–38, an international Marian magazine; but here I shall confine myself to remarks illustrative of the misunderstanding of critical NT exegesis on the part of an ultraconservative scholar, comparable to the misunderstanding illustrated above on the part of a liberal scholar.

The book is openly hostile to modern historical-critical exegesis of the NT, and advanced promotion for the English edition suggested broadly that it would save readers from all the nefarious mythologizing of the infancy gospels that has been going on. Usually one cannot hold authors responsible for promotional overstatements, but in this instance Laurentin's own affirmations are not much less inflammatory. It may help readers to know that Laurentin wrote a foreword to George Kelly's attack on biblical critics in the *New Biblical Theorists*, a book which an Irish scholar described as ''thinly veiled animosity, incessant slurs, bitter pervasive righteousness.''[68] Laurentin has also praised a French attack on current Gospel exegesis by Claude Tresmontant, a book that has been refuted severely by P. Grelot,[69] a distinguished French NT exegete and a member of the Pontifical Biblical Commission.

In his infancy narrative book Laurentin begins by lamenting the sad state of Roman Catholic Church life in which priests initiated hastily into

---

[67]*Les Evangiles de l'Enfance du Christ* (Paris: Desclée, 1982; 2nd ed. 1983); *The Truth of Christmas beyond the Myths* (Still River, MA: St. Bede's, 1985). Promoters of the English translation were turned down by a number of reputable publishers; a falsehood was then circulated that I was attempting to block an English edition. I was in Rome on sabbatical while these transactions were going on; I had not even read the book, and no publisher contacted me or asked my opinion before turning it down.

[68]J. Murphy-O'Connor, *TBT* 22 (#2; March 1984) 110; Bishop Richard J. Sklba in *CBQ* 46 (1984) 576–77 states that Kelly ''has not written a good book''; his ''use of sources seems hurried and superficial''; his ''1946 doctorate in social sciences has not equipped him for entry into the discussion.''

[69]*Evangiles et Tradition Apostolique* (Paris: Cerf, 1984); he devotes pp. 161–63 to ''a strange praise'' of Tresmontant by Laurentin, politely wondering how Laurentin could laud such a book. I have commented on the ultraconservative extreme in French Catholic exegesis in ''All Gaul Is Divided,'' *Union Seminary Quarterly Review* 40 (1985) 99–103.

what pretends to be a scientific exegesis do not dare to preach any more about the basic gospel of Christmas, knowing that it is a myth. A "scientific" reductionism which had its origin in the rationalism of the last century has been taken up belatedly by Catholics, so that today rationalist presuppositions have won over a large part of the ecclesiastical intelligentsia.[70] In other words, while Sheehan had a "liberal consensus" of exegetes and theologians, Laurentin has a rationalist consensus among Catholic exegetes. Laurentin is less generous than Sheehan in listing the rationalist exegetes who attack the infancy gospels largely because they do not believe in the miraculous. But certainly he refers with negative frequency to both J. A. Fitzmyer and to me; and so once again the rationalist consensus (if we may use the term) seems to include people that Rome has selected for the Pontifical Biblical Commission. All this means to Laurentin that an ecumenical harmony in agreement with his earlier view of Marian symbolism is being undone.[71]

As I read Laurentin's analysis, I had five reactions: (1) I do not think that the discussion is helped by the extremely pejorative terminology employed by Laurentin. Several times he describes an opponent as rabid, (*acharné*),[72] when one might well find the style of Laurentin to be rabid. For instance, in the short span of 12 pages in the French (439–51) he accomplishes the following feats of vituperation. He describes one of my views, which other scholars discuss seriously, as a hypothesis that, at the profit of "an imagination without foundation," departs from the precise information given in the text. He describes various historical theories of the composition of the Lucan canticles as an immoderate taste for fiction and the novel, as caricatures and simplistic, as fragile and incoherent. The nadir of such oratory comes on page 439 where certain critical hypotheses about the infancy narratives are characterized as "the excrement of historical research." Such language is not appropriate to scholarly discourse.

(2) In my own country, I have encountered very few priests who do not preach the Christmas gospel. It is quite true that many of them preach a simplistic and even saccharine sentimentality about the Baby Jesus; but certainly they are not afraid to mention the contents of Christ-

---

[70]Laurentin, *Evangiles* 8–9, 455.

[71]*Evangiles* 9, 59.

[72]*Evangiles* 68 ("l'acharnement"), 375 ("On s'est acharné").

mas. As for the supposedly deleterious effects of historical criticism, is it immodest for me to mention that in response to *BM* I received many letters from both Protestant and Catholic preachers thanking me for offering them much material, especially by way of background and OT information, that enabled them to enrich their preaching of the Gospel passages?

(3) As I read Laurentin' sweeping condemnation of Catholic exegetes, I wondered who precisely were those who have been converted to positivism, rationalism, and idealism? Among the highly esteemed historical-critical NT exegetes in Catholicism today, I would think immediately in Germany, of Schnackenburg, Vögtle, Gnilka, and Kertelge; in Austria, of Kremer; in Switzerland, of Ruckstuhl and Barthélemy; in France, of Léon-Dufour and Grelot; in Belgium, of Neirynck and Dupont; in Italy, of Ghiberti; in India, of L. Legrand; in the USA, of Fitzmyer, Senior, Meier, Karris, Pheme Perkins, etc. (I am sure that I have done an injustice to many others whose names have not come immediately to my mind.) Has Laurentin evidence that a single one of these people is a rationalist, an idealist, or a positivist? Are their books of critical exegesis filled with a denial of the supernatural and religious? It is surprising to find sweeping, undocumented charges against Catholic exegetes in what purports to be a scholarly investigation.

(4) I am puzzled by the claim of Laurentin that Catholic critical exegesis in general, and of the infancy narratives in particular, is prejudiced by a systematic suspicion of the miraculous. I know of none of the above-mentioned scholars who deny the miraculous; and in *BM* (p. 188) I explicitly rejected as unscientific the presupposition that miracles are impossible. Does Laurentin's charge about the denial of the miraculous disguise the fact that the problems that I and others have with the historicity of the infancy narratives have nothing to do with rationalist presuppositions?

(5) It is surprising to read that the mariological symbolism of Laurentin's earlier work won much ecumenical support. In the French (p. 59), Laurentin mentions in this connection one French Catholic (Lyonnet, 1939), one Scandinavian Lutheran (Sahlin, 1946), one Anglican (Hebert, 1950) and one French Reformed (Thurian, 1962). Certainly, as I have mentioned above, many aspects of Laurentin's OT symbolism were widely accepted in Catholicism but not, as a matter of fact, in German and American Protestantism. If one reflects on the fact that German

and American scholarship constitute the backbone of the classical Protestant position, he can scarcely claim an ecumenical consensus. In particular, Laurentin does not debate in detail the ecumenically sponsored
and published book *MNT* which disagrees with his views and supports a
critical approach to the infancy narratives—a book done by American
Catholics and Protestants (Lutheran, Reformed, Anglican) and subsequently translated into German, Spanish, and Italian (forthcoming). Is
this book not a sign of an ecumenical consensus which never existed before and is emerging through critical biblical exegesis? Or is such a work
not a consensus because Laurentin does not agree with it?

*   *   *

Let me move on now from observations about Laurentin's outlook
on the general state of historical-critical exegesis in Roman Catholicism
to some comments about his attitudes toward infancy narrative research.
Here his antipathy expresses itself in the language he uses to describe the
works with which he disagrees. Quotation marks often set off the terms
"criticism" and "critical" to suggest to the reader that the writing so
designated is not really critical or scientific. His standard term for the
theories of biblical critics is "presuppositions," sometimes with the
added specification "fragile." This term suggests that the historical critics have made up their minds about many issues before they approach
the evidence. (A sadly amusing comment on this terminology is Laurentin's own massive presupposition which he never identifies as such,
namely, the unprovable assumption that Mary lived on in the Jerusalem
community and could have been the indirect source of the information
in the infancy narratives.) If critics point to a lack of *verifiable* historicity
in the infancy narratives, Laurentin deems them to be proposing "creation," "fiction" or "fabricated explication,"[73] whether or not such
terminology is used by the authors themselves. Laurentin's especially
favored terminology for an approach that does not affirm historicity is
to describe it as reducing the narrative to a "theologoumenon," not recognizing that thus he often misrepresents the views of his opponents.
Although I rarely used the word in *BM*,[74] on p. 505 I had this note:

---

[73]*Evangiles* 442, 445, 447, 461, etc.
[74]My index gives six instances although there may be a few more.

"Scholars use 'theologoumenon' in various ways, but I am using it in the sense indicated [the historicizing of what was originally a theological statement]." Notice I did not say: *fictional* historicizing. Nevertheless, when he criticizes me and others, Laurentin always is accusing us of reducing the passage to fiction, for he relates the theologoumenon language to Hegel's historical rationalism.[75]

Thus, in reporting views with which he disagrees, Laurentin often hardens the presentation to the point of distortion. For instance, he states (French, p. 20) that according to my *BM,* Luke would have introduced the Magnificat at a later period into the infancy narrative precisely in order to "revalue" Mary, in the process of forging the theologoumenon of 1:28–56. By "revalue" Laurentin means that I considered that the value given to Mary was fictional. In my hypothesis that Luke had introduced the Canticles of the infancy narrative at a later stage, however, I took pains to insist that the Canticles (which I thought came from an early Jewish-Christian community, probably in Jerusalem) *fitted* the characters to whom they were attributed in the infancy narrative (*BM,* p. 349). Therefore, there is no question of the Magnificat giving a value that was not there. Also, I did *not* state in my book that the annunciation was a theologoumenon. Since Laurentin defines a theologoumenon as a fictional creation, it is noteworthy that I affirmed just the opposite, specifically rejecting the designations of fiction and theologoumenon for the contents of the annunciation scene in Luke. In *BM* (p. 527) I rejected as unlikely the thesis that the virginal conception was a theological dramatization or a fictional creation. On p. 308 I wrote, "I do not regard the theologoumenon interpretation of the virginal conception as adequate." I stated on p. 347 that the attribution of the Magnificat to Mary "is not a question of a purely fictional creation, for the dramatis personae are remembered or conceived of as representative of a certain type of piety which the Canticles vocalize . . . Moreover, the Canticles pick up and continue motifs that were in the infancy narrative pertinent to the three speakers." Thus, I am very far from turning 1:28–56 into a theologoumenon or fiction. Indeed, the constant introduction of the theme of fiction into Laurentin's presentation of my views and those of others is misleading. There is an enormous range between historicity and pure fiction. For instance, basic facts may have developed in a popular, imag-

---

[75]*Evangiles* 593, 115.

inative, poetic way that removes the final narratives from the category
of history, but does *not* leave them in the categories of creation or fiction.
Incidentally, I may mention that in the brief treatment of Laurentin by
Grelot (footnote 69 above), there is a critique of *Les Evangiles* on this
precise point. Even beyond the issue of theologoumenon and fiction, Laurentin's
misrepresentation of the views of those whom he opposes is serious and,
I believe, is related to a fundamental misunderstanding of the precision
of historical criticism. Let me list a number of the misrepresentations in
almost telegraphic fashion. In each case I will put the page number of
the French volume, the misrepresentation, and a brief correction of it:

- P. 82, 472: J. A. Fitzmyer is "more radical" than I on the virginal
  conception because he holds that the evangelists did not consider the
  virginal conception to be a reality. *Comment:* In fact, Fitzmyer never
  questioned that Matthew regarded the virginal conception as a reality
  and now in his Anchor Bible Commentary on Luke (p. 338) he agrees
  with me that Luke probably considered it to be a reality—Laurentin
  knows this book well.

- P. 447: Laurentin says that Fitzmyer found my view that the Magnificat
  may have been placed on the lips of Mary as "forced." *Comment:* Fitzmyer, Anchor Bible p. 361, wrote that he found my view "forceful."

- P. 370: Laurentin writes that Brown in his research on the infancy narratives posed as a principle, "Mary is not historical but symbolical."
  Comment: I have never written or made that statement, and Laurentin's
  footnote to *BRCFC* 84–87 where I *was quoting Pannenberg* neglects
  the qualifications that I brought to Pannenberg's idea when I summa-
  rized on 104–8. I stated there and I affirm now that the NT does not
  give us much knowledge of Mary as a historical character and for that
  reason she lends herself more freely than Jesus does to a symbolic trajectory, so that symbolism may be a more fruitful approach to Mary
  than history. None of that makes her non-historical or a pure symbol,
  and none of it constitutes a principle of exegesis. My principle of exegesis is the meaning of the texts of Matthew and Luke whether or not
  they have anything to do with Mary.

- P. 484: Brown contends that the virginal conception appeared only in
  the two Gospels from the last third of the first century. *Comment:* I
  have written extensively that the agreement of these two Gospels on

the virginal conception means that this idea antedated both Matthew and Luke and therefore was an early understanding by Christians.

■ P. 472: Although Brown accepts the virginal conception, he raises the question of whether or not it was a fictional theologoumenon. *Comment:* Laurentin might have told his readers that I said it was not a theologoumenon.

■ P. 429: *BM* is an improvement on Brown's earlier work, but Brown does not know whether Jesus was born of a virgin or of Joseph. *Comment:* This contradicts what I wrote in *BM*, pp. 527–29, namely, that I remain convinced of the conclusions I reached in my earlier works and that the NT evidence favors the historicity of the virginal conception, and that consistent church teaching in support of that historicity is an extremely important and even deciding factor in this issue. It is startling that Laurentin says that I do not know whether Jesus was born of a virgin or of Joseph since I affirmed twice in *BM* (pp. 9, 484) that I accept Roman Catholic faith and church dogma on Mary.

■ P. 442: Although Brown allows a pre-gospel tradition behind the annunciation, he thinks that that scene gives no information about revelation received by Mary; for Brown it is an explanation fabricated by the evangelist for the reader, a fabrication that denies to Mary any real vocation or response to God. *Comment:* In *BM*, pp. 526–27, although I indicated that the annunciation by an angel is a figurative way of describing divine revelation, in no way did I deny that Mary received a revelation. I added that the scene involved Luke's application of statements reflecting what he knew about Mary from the gospel account of the ministry—scarcely a fabrication! Laurentin makes no distinction between Mary's receiving a revelation and my indication that I do not know if she was able to formulate that revelation in the way it is now found in Luke 1.

■ P. 54: Brown's picture of the development of christology in the NT involves a prefabricated scheme divinizing Christ. *Comment:* In *BM*, pp. 30 and 134, I wrote that "Christians reflected further on the mystery of Jesus' identity," insisting that such retrospective evaluation involved the "appreciation of a reality that was already there." I carefully pointed out that there was no question of changing the reality of who Jesus was but only of finding the theological vocabulary to express it. Never have I used any language suggesting the divinizing of Christ.

WHY AND WITH WHAT RESULTS?

I trust that the above examples show that, on the ultraconservative end of the spectrum, Laurentin is just as inept as Sheehan was on the liberal end of the spectrum in reporting the nuances of historical criticism. (In an appendix I shall critique Laurentin's own exegesis, but I am concerned here with the failure to appreciate and use correctly the contributions of Roman Catholic historical critics.) McHugh asked how to relate to Catholic dogma the observations of historical-critical exegetes about the infancy narratives and about Mary (if one accepts them—and often McHugh does not). That is a perfectly valid inquiry; and, as I indicated, I have tried in Chapter 2 to meet the issue. But Laurentin sees a rationalist consensus of Catholic exegetes who have become the heirs of Hegel. Thus, like Sheehan, he has woven his understanding of what Catholic scholars are saying into his preconceptions (see pp. 62-63 above). Disturbed by the *surface novelty* of infancy narrative research (the observation that there may be limited historicity), he has not grasped the *deeper novelty,* namely, that this observation does not detract from the doctrinal import or spiritual utility of the infancy gospels. He has (explicitly or implicitly) superimposed on the issue two false "presuppositions." First, if the narratives are not (directly or indirectly) substantially accurate family history, for Laurentin they are fictional creations. Actually, there is a whole range of intermediary possibilities between fact and fiction, e.g., some historical facts such as descent from David, conception through the Holy Spirit, holiness of the parents, and upbringing at Nazareth may have been the subject of reflection in the light of OT motifs—the end product, without being either history or fiction, would have consisted of profound insights into the importance of Jesus' origins for an understanding of his identity. This leads us to Laurentin's second false "presupposition": since Christianity is a historical religion, the infancy narratives lose much or all of their value if they are not historical in most details. The historicity of Christianity, however, is related to the factual reality of *the main salvific deeds* of Jesus' life: his birth, his preaching, his acts of healing power, his crucifixion, and resurrection. This historicity does *not* demand that the Gospels be literal and factual in all details; the Pontifical Biblical Commission's statement (pp. 12-14 above) has made that clear.

Precisely because I see the virginal conception (and perhaps even

Davidic descent) as essential to the salvific story of Jesus, I have argued that we may invoke the ordinary teaching of the church as a guide on the historicity of that particular fact. In contending that one should not interpret an essential relationship to salvation so broadly as to cover most details in the infancy narratives, I was stressing that issues of historicity are not the key to the importance of these narratives. Debates about historicity often concern matters quite foreign to the emphasis of the evangelists themselves, and so in *BM* I confined such debates largely to appendixes. (It is a disturbing indication of the proclivities of ultraconservative reviewers that often in commenting on *BM* they devoted most of their time to the relatively short appendixes and ignored the lengthy text of the commentary.) I spent most of my effort on a positive analysis of the tremendous wealth of the infancy narratives, so evocative of the OT and so brilliantly clear on the christology of Jesus as the Son of God. I would argue that, in a misguided effort to save the infancy narratives from a danger that does *not* exist in the writing of many responsible Roman Catholic exegetes, Laurentin in his latest book really takes the regressive step of forcing us to debate historicity over and over again, since most value in his outlook depends on that historicity. Whether or not he intended it, his book is already being lionized by extremist Roman Catholics opposed to the openings in biblical criticism sponsored by the church itself.[76]

---

[76]Propaganda misuse is also being made of the preface of one-and-a-half pages written for the second edition by Cardinal Joseph Ratzinger, Prefect of the Roman Congregation for the Doctrine of the Faith. Recognizing that Vatican II shows us the importance of biblical criticism, the Cardinal justifiably criticizes those who reduce the infancy narratives to pure imagery without any historical reality and eventually without theological value. (See my comments to the same effect in *VCBRJ* 23–27 and *BM* 7, 37.) The Cardinal praises the contributions of Laurentin's earlier book of 1956, even as I did on p. 74 above. In the last nine lines of the preface the Cardinal turns to the present book with the non-committal wish that it find attentive readers. I agree fully with the need for *attentive* reading, for care will show that this book is inferior to Laurentin's earlier work. His generalizations, accusing responsible Catholic scholars of rationalism and fictionalizing, will be a source of confusion and division. J. A. Fitzmyer, whom Laurentin has criticized as "more radical" than I, and P. Grelot, who has disagreed with Laurentin's dichotomy between history and fiction, have recently been appointed to the Roman Pontifical Biblical Commission with Cardinal Ratzinger's approval. Thus the Cardinal's preface does *not* constitute a blanket approval of Laurentin's ideas and polemic, despite promotional claims being made to that effect.

Perhaps I can close by two lists that exemplify in a most concrete fashion the problem I see presented by René Laurentin. The first list will concern historicity; the second list will concern the value of the infancy narratives.

If I read correctly, because Laurentin thinks the infancy narratives came to us directly or indirectly from family tradition (especially from Mary), he would in some way regard the following details as substantially historical:

- Angels appeared to Mary and Joseph.
- Mary and Joseph originally lived in Nazareth.
- A census under Quirinius brought them to Bethlehem.
- A star was interpreted by magi from the East as the sign of the birth of the King of the Jews, and they came to Bethlehem and found the child.
- Angels appeared to shepherds.
- The four Lucan infancy Canticles (*Magnificat, Benedictus, Nunc Dimittis, Gloria in Excelsis*) were in whole or part uttered by those to whom Luke attributes them.
- Herod learned about the birth of Jesus and slaughtered children at Bethlehem.
- Mary and Joseph fled to Egypt.

By way of difference from Laurentin, historical-critical study of the infancy narratives leads me and many other Roman Catholic exegetes to be very uncertain about the historicity of the above listed details for the reasons I gave on pp. 67-69 above. Notice: I do not say that I think most or all of these details are not historical; I affirm that I have no exegetical way of knowing that they are historical, and nothing in the way of church teaching or theology resolves this problem for me. In order words, I affirm that the question of the historicity or non-historicity of such details is a matter of good scholarship, rather than of Catholic faith, or of Christian identity, or of love for Christ and Mary. If Laurentin or any other ultraconservative thinks that the matters I just listed above are objects of Catholic faith, proof has to be supplied.

Now let me give a second list of issues on which Laurentin and I *agree,* irrespective of our differences about the historicity of the first list:

- The infancy narratives are true gospel: magnificent narratives, with deep theology and spirituality.

- They give us a sensitive, poetic understanding of the history of salvation, relating the story of Jesus to the OT.
- They should not become the victims of rationalism and should not be treated simply as fiction, fable, or myth (in the popular sense of that term).
- They give us a splendidly high christology of Jesus as Son of God, and their common emphasis on the virginal conception of Jesus is an intrinsic part of the Catholic faith.
- They supply an essential component to the Christian mariological tradition, portraying Mary as specially chosen by God in His plan of salvation, as conceiving her child by the power of the Holy Spirit, as the one to whom the unique identity of Jesus was first revealed, and as the first one to respond to that good news according to the basic criterion of discipleship (hearing the word of God and doing it).
- They follow the proclamation of the identity of Jesus with another essential aspect of the gospel, namely, God's grace making sure that this good news is shared with others, Jews and Gentiles.

To my mind, this second list describes what is really important in the infancy narratives for Christian faith, Catholic dogma, and spirituality. To those open to persuasion it should clearly demonstrate the fallacy of driving a wedge between modern biblical exegesis and the traditional doctrinal proclamation of the church.

Chapter 5
THE CONTRIBUTION OF CRITICAL EXEGESIS TO AN UNDERSTANDING OF MARY AND MARIAN DOCTRINE

The last two chapters, while necessary, do not really touch the heart of the issue I am discussing in this book. To appreciate the relationship between critical exegesis and doctrine, misunderstandings must be removed; but the ultimate test is positive rather than negative. Are we richer in our appreciation of Christian realities because Catholic biblical scholars are using historical-critical exegesis? I maintain that we are, and in this chapter I shall put my contention to the test by showing how critical scholarship presents Mary, the mother of Jesus. I hope to show that solid critical exegesis promotes a mariology defensible both by Scripture and Tradition. Mariology is almost a bellwether indicating theological direction in the Roman Catholic Church today. Curiously, the extremely conservative and the extremely liberal are in agreement that Marian devotion is irreconcilable with the theology that has come to the fore since Vatican II. The answer of the extreme conservatives is to get rid of recent theology; the answer of the extreme liberals is to get rid of mariology. The ability of post-Vatican II theology to preserve what is of worth in mariology and give it new life is a test of validity, since in Roman Catholicism we have never built our theology by destroying what went before, nor have we made theological progress simply by repeating what went before. The intelligent ability to preserve the best of the past and apply it to new situations is an important factor in judging whether theology is truly catholic.

In seeking to show the doctrinal benefits of applying critical exegesis to a scriptural study of Mary, I shall follow the line of development illustrated in a work I have already mentioned, *MNT,* done by Christian scholars of various churches.[77] I was involved in editing this mariological study, commissioned by the American Catholic Bishops' Commission for Ecumenical Affairs and by the Lutheran Churches as a contribution to a larger study on papal authority. An instance of papal authority that particularly disturbed Protestants was the definition of the Marian dogmas, the Immaculate Conception and the Assumption. It was felt that if Protestants and Catholics could agree on what the NT said about Mary, there might be some way of judging whether the exercise of papal authority in regard to those doctrines had a basis in Scripture, or was quite alien to Scripture.

As we met and studied the Scriptures, it became apparent that because Protestants and Catholics had not worked over Marian texts together, we were somewhat ignorant of the operative texts of Scripture in the minds of the other party. (Basically most church use of Scripture is selective; and often a difference between Protestants and Roman Catholics is not a lack of loyalty of either party to the Scriptures, but a greater loyalty to some sections of the Scriptures over others.) And so when we began to discuss which texts should be discussed first, some of the Protestants suggested that we should study the Marcan texts, while immediately some Catholics thought of the Lucan texts. I reflected that John McHugh's 500-page *The Mother of Jesus in the New Testament* (p. 69 above) had never seriously treated the basic Marcan text on Mary—a sign of just how alien Mark's voice on Mary was for Catholics. Yet it also became obvious that some of our Protestant confreres had never really looked at the Lucan texts independently of Mark. Obviously we had to agree to look at *all* the Marian texts in the NT if we were to allow Scripture to challenge our divisive presuppositions.

---

[77] I shall present in this chapter my own views succinctly; those interested in the argumentation and documentation behind these views will find *MNT* very useful.

THE PAULINE EPISTLES

We turned first of all to the oldest works in the NT, Paul's undisputed letters. It is startling to find that Mary is never mentioned by Paul. True, there is a reference to Christ who is God's Son, *born of a woman, born under the Law* (Gal 4:4). But when some Catholics look at that as a Marian text, there is astonishment among Protestants, as well there might be. Being "born of a woman" happens to be one heritage that all human beings share, and constituted a common expression in Judaism for a human being. When Jesus wants to praise John the Baptist he says, "Among those born of women, no one is greater than he" (Matt 11:11). Though some try to shape an argument based on the verb in Galatians for a reference to virgin birth (no *man* mentioned), the genius of the text is against it. Paul is talking about Christ who is human and Jewish. He is born of a woman and so is a human being; and he is born under the Law and so is a Jew—that gives the categories in which Jesus operates. He is God's Son, truly human and truly Jewish, who is going to bring salvation to all human beings, to Jews first and then to Gentiles. The text never reflects on the mother of Jesus (see MNT 42-43).

When we realize that the great Apostle of the Gentiles could preach the gospel and yet not mention Mary, it does remind us that in a certain sense, the heart of the gospel could find a non-mariological expression. Now I am very aware that Paul's corpus of letters is not a total indication of Paul's mind and I would not want to draw any absolutely negative conclusions about Paul's knowledge of Mary. But at least we who have found Mary so useful and necessary for our articulation of the gospel may gain a sense of why others can say they do not experience that need. Granted the dominant place of Paul in the Protestant mind, we get a sense of why Protestant thought patterns about Mary sometimes do not move in the same way as ours.

Actually, the only NT mentions of Mary are in the four Gospels, plus one reference in the Book of Acts. (The latter reference, occurring just before Pentecost, describes the early community, consisting of the eleven minus Judas, the women who were at the tomb, and the *mother* and brothers of Jesus.) So then, mariological research must concentrate on the Gospel accounts of the public ministry of Jesus and ultimately on Matthew's and Luke's birth stories. We know not a single NT detail about Mary in history after Pentecost; her role is in the lifetime of Jesus.

It is even more sobering to find that in the first three Gospels she appears only *once* during the public ministry.

THE GOSPEL ACCORDING TO MARK

Let us begin with the Marcan account of the scene, a very difficult account for Roman Catholics. We are told in Mark 3:31–35:

> His mother and his brothers came; and standing outside they sent to him and called him. A crowd was sitting around him; and they said to him, "Your mother and your brothers are outside, asking for you." Jesus replied, "Who are my mother and my brothers?" And looking about at those who sat around him, he said, "Here are my mother and my brothers. Whoever does the will of God is brother and sister and mother to me."

Now, in part, it is *the intrinsic staging* of the scene that makes it so offensive. The mother and the brothers, the family by birth, are outside. Jesus is inside and has gathered disciples around him. When they report that his mother and brothers are outside, he asks, "Who are my mother and my brothers?" And looking about on those who were sitting around him he says, "Here are my mother and brothers." There is not only a definition but a distinction. Jesus deliberately points to those inside, not to those outside, "Whoever does the will of God is brother and sister and mother to me." We are encountering the radicalism of Jesus. He comes among a people where everything depends on birth, for it is characteristic of Judaism that one is a member of God's people by being born of a Jewish mother. The radical challenge of Jesus is that birth does not bring about significant relationship. What accomplishes this and makes a true family is doing the will of God as he proclaims it. There is no indication in Mark that Jesus thinks of his mother and brothers in the category of family constituted by doing the will of God. Mark does not exclude them, but he distinguishes natural birth relationship from this new family relationship.

The Marian import of the scene is made more difficult because of *the Marcan setting*. Mark has reported the calling of the Twelve, after which Jesus has gone to Capernaum by the lake which is now his base of operations. His home was originally in the mountains of Galilee around Nazareth, but he does not go up there. Rather, he begins to use Peter's home, where the mother-in-law was healed, as a center for the ministry. His preaching attracts such crowds that he does not even get time to eat. Mark reports, "When *his own* heard this, they set out to seize him; for they said, 'He is beside himself' " (3:21). And then Mark has a scene where scribes come down from Jerusalem and say that Jesus is possessed by Beelzebul. After Jesus answers them, the mother and brothers arrive asking for him (3:31–35). Such a pattern reflects Marcan style. Mark will start a scene of movement to a place. (Jesus starts out to heal the daughter of Jairus in 5:23–24.) In order to fill in the interval of the journey, Mark has an intervening scene which tells of something that happens along the way. (The woman in the crowd touches Jesus and is healed in 5:25–34.) And then we are told what happened at the end of the journey. (Jesus arrives at the house of Jairus and heals the daughter in 5:35–43.) In Marcan criticism we call this (ungracefully) the "sandwich technique." There is a beginning to which one comes back at the end, and sandwiched in between is an intervening scene. Applied to Mark 3:21–35, the pattern begins with "his own" who think he is beside himself and set out to seize him; next there is the intervening scene about Beelzebul. (*His own* think he is beside himself; *his enemies* think he is possessed by the devil.) Finally his mother and brothers arrive. Probably, then, Mark thinks that the mother and brothers are "his own," i.e., his own relatives who think he is beside himself and do not understand him at all. Thus Mark contrasts both "his own" (who do not understand him) and his enemies (who think he is possessed by the devil) with Jesus' disciples who hear the word of God and do it. That is the only scene in Mark in which the mother of Jesus ever appears, and one must admit it is not a scene that would incline one to develop a great devotion to the mother of Jesus. Yet that is the basic biblical text which many Protestants (perhaps in reaction to Catholicism) associate with Mary.

There is one other mention of Mary in the Marcan Gospel, when Jesus goes back to Nazareth (6:1–6). As Jesus begins to teach in the synagogue, the local people are astonished. They ask, "Well now, where did this fellow get all this . . . wisdom? Isn't he a carpenter? Isn't he the son of Mary and the brother of James and Joses and Judas and Simon? Are not his sisters here with us?" They took offense at the local carpenter-boy turned preacher. And Jesus said to them, "A prophet is not without honor except in his own country, among his own relatives, and in his own house." If one retranslates the negation, Jesus is *not honored* in his own country, *among his own relatives,* and in his own house. Again Mark offers us no beginning of a trajectory or line of development in mariology.

Yet such an attitude toward Jesus' family is part of Mark's starkness. Mark presents a Gospel in which Jesus is alone and misunderstood. He is not understood by his disciples; he is not understood by Peter; he is not understood by his relatives; and he is certainly not understood by his enemies. The Marcan Gospel stresses the suffering and misunderstanding that Jesus had to go through in order to make clear that there is no other way to know Jesus except through the cross. Such a Gospel has intense power and is a very important part of the Christian message; yet in another sense it presents an inadequate picture. By so stressing what one must go through in order to understand Jesus, Mark does not do justice to what happens to those who finally do understand Jesus. Neither Matthew nor Luke (who, I presuppose, knew Mark) were satisfied with the Marcan picture—that is part of the reason why Matthew and Luke wrote their own Gospels. The changing of Mark implicit in Matthew and Luke is understandable once we appreciate that every biblical book is limited by the circumstances in which it was written. The word of God was phrased by human beings who dealt with certain issues and had limited perceptions. When one asks biblical books for perceptions that were not theirs, one is ignoring the limitation of Scripture. Matthew and Luke are not content to preach the gospel without showing how it transformed the people who surrounded Jesus. The gospel thus becomes a story of Jesus *with believers around him*—not yet total believers, but people whose lives are already being changed by their contact with him. For that reason the Matthean view of Peter differs from the Marcan view of Peter, and similarly with Mary. Matthew (as a well as Luke) knows something about Jesus that Mark seems to be ignorant of, namely that Jesus was conceived virginally of Mary by divine power. That is Matthew's (and Luke's) contribution to Christian memory. The insight that God was already at work in this woman in the conception of Jesus begins to transform the understanding of how Mary reacted to Jesus. In Matthew there is a moderate transformation; in Luke the transformation is dramatic.

THE GOSPEL ACCORDING TO MATTHEW

Briefly, in the Matthean infancy story Joseph is the main figure, while Mary is mentioned only in her role as the mother of the child through the power of the Spirit. The main drama concerns Joseph, how he appropriates the angelic message in obedience to God's word, and how he saves the divine child. But knowing that Mary conceived through the Holy Spirit causes Matthew to change the Marcan ministry scene of the mother and brothers of Jesus (Matt 12:46–50). Matthew in 12:22–50 has parallels to everything in Mark 3:19–35 with the *exception* of Mark 3:19–21 where "his own" say, "He is beside himself." Matthew must have understood Mark to refer to the mother and family of Jesus; and Matthew cannot allow that a mother who conceived Jesus through the Holy Spirit could so misunderstand him. When Matthew (13:53–58) comes to the scene where Jesus goes back to Nazareth and the village people ask where he got his wisdom, Matthew makes two significant changes. First, always more reverential than Mark, Matthew does not have Jesus called a carpenter but "the son of a carpenter." (By the way, the whole imagery of Joseph as a carpenter rests on this Matthean change of Mark, the only reference to Joseph's trade in the NT.) Second, Matthew phrases Jesus' words thus: "A prophet is not without honor except in his own country and in his own house," *leaving out* "among his own relatives." It is inconceivable to Matthew that the woman who conceived this child through the power of God would not honor her son. One begins to see how the Christian understanding of God's plan begins to color the picture of Mary.

THE GOSPEL ACCORDING TO LUKE

An even more dramatic change in the development of Marian thought comes in Luke. Unlike Matthew's infancy narrative which concentrates on Joseph and tells us about the just man, Luke's infancy narrative concentrates totally on Mary. The story is told from her perspective and, of course, the central part of it concerns the annunciation and birth of the child. Her life is totally filled with the good news that Christ is coming.

I am going to come back to this section when I speak about our Lady of Guadalupe (p. 98 below). But for the moment I simply call attention to the basic message of the angel who appears to the Virgin Mary and tells her (using Davidic language from II Sam 7:12–16) that the child is going to be the Son of David. Mary brings up the human obstacle that she is a virgin, not having had relations with a man; the angel is thus given the opportunity to explain how this child will be conceived. The Holy Spirit will come upon her; the power of the Most High will over-shadow her; and so the child will be the Son of God. Thus Mary learns that the Son of David and the Son of God is to be born to her. There follows the visitation to Elizabeth where she is hailed as mother of the Lord. Mary's *Magnificat,* to which I shall return, reminds us of the cen-trality of Mary in the story. In the birth narrative of Luke, the shepherds come and find the child with *Mary,* the mother. Similarly Mary is central in the presentation in the Temple and later in the finding of Jesus at age twelve. Mary is constantly center stage.

Such a narrative concentration on Mary, plus the description of her as saying, ''Be it done unto me according to your word,'' gives Mary a unique status. In our ecumenical discussion, we saw that, according to the criterion of discipleship based on doing the will of God, the Lucan Mary becomes the first Christian disciple (see footnote 40 above). Once Mary meets the qualifications of discipleship, the Gospel portrayal of her becomes radically different. Luke is not unconscious that discipleship is an ongoing lifetime process. And so he warns, in the words of Simeon (2:33–35), that through Mary's soul too the sword of division must pierce. Every person must face the sword of deciding what doing the word of God means, a sword that divides the believer from the non-believer. In facing the sword, the Lucan Mary was on the positive side all through Jesus' life and beyond. When Luke comes to the one scene in the common tradition where Mary appears in the ministry (Luke 8:19–21 = Mark 3:31–35), like Matthew he leaves out the Marcan introduc-tion (Mark 3:21). It is inconceivable to Luke that Jesus' ''own'' (family) would not comprehend him. More significantly and unlike Matthew, Luke radically transforms the Marcan form of the scene where the mother of Jesus comes with the brothers asking for him. In Mark we saw an unfavorable distinction between the natural family and a family of believers. In Luke also the mother and brothers come and stand outside, asking for Jesus. But when Jesus is told, ''Your mother and brothers are standing outside, desiring to see you,'' he does *not* ask, ''Who are my mother and my brothers?'' He does *not* point to those inside as his mother and brothers. Rather he affirms in response, "My mother and brothers are those who hear the word of God and do it." That is a highly significant change. There is no longer a contrast between a family of believers and a natural family—to the contrary, the natural family now become exemplary believers. Jesus' mother and brothers who stand outside are those who hear the word of God and do it, and thus are examples of what discipleship should be. In the annunciation Mary was the first one to hear the word and to do it; she continues to be presented in the ministry as the example of those who hear and do.

As for the setting of this appearance of Mary in the ministry of Jesus (her only appearance), Luke moves it later in the Gospel after the parable of the sower and the seed (8:19–21 following 8:4–15). The seed that falls on good soil and bears fruit a hundredfold consists of "those who, hearing the word, hold it fast." Six verses later Jesus says, "My mother and my brothers are those who hear the word of God and do it," so that they become examples of the seed in good ground. Luke remains consistent to the picture of the mother and brothers as fruitful disciples when, at the beginning of the Book of Acts (1:14) between the ascension and Pentecost, he places them alongside the eleven, and the women (who observed the burial of the crucified Jesus)—the believing community Jesus left behind. Mary was the first one to hear the gospel even before Jesus' birth; during the ministry she was praised as one of those who hear the word of God and do it; and after the death, resurrection, and ascension of Jesus she is shown as having remained faithful, waiting for the Spirit. Thus she serves as the most consistent disciple in the whole gospel narrative. This is a tremendous development in the line of the NT reflection on Mary. The development comes after Mark was written and begins to move us toward what will happen in the subsequent church.

THE GOSPEL ACCORDING TO JOHN

More evidence about this line of development may be found in John which goes its own way, presenting a tradition different from that in the first three Gospels. John is not interested in the natural birth of Jesus, and so there is no infancy narrative. But there are two scenes in which the mother of Jesus appears. Neither of these is an exact parallel of the one public-ministry scene in the Synoptic tradition; but each of them in its own way reflects the same theme as the Synoptic scene.

At Cana Jesus is among family. His mother attends a wedding as do his brothers (2:1,12)—evidently a wedding of friends of the family. His mother puts a request, seemingly with an awareness of Jesus' extraordinary powers on which she places a family claim, to help her friends who are out of wine. We note the resemblance to the Lucan scene of Jesus at age twelve. There Mary says, ''Your father and I have sought you sorrowing. Why have you done this to us?'' That too is a family claim on him whose priorities come from another source. Jesus' answer to the mother who says, ''Your father and I have sought you sorrowing,'' is that she should have known that he would be ''about my Father's business.'' His real father is not Mary's spouse, and God has a priority over human family relationship. The same theme appears in the Johannine Cana scene. When the mother places her demand, Jesus replies, ''What has that business of yours to do with me? My hour has not yet come.'' He has a different set of priorities established by his heavenly Father and not by natural family claims. And yet, Mary is not shown as she is in Mark, as an outsider. Already at Cana the portrait begins to shade over into the more positive picture of Matthew and Luke. Even though Jesus has rebuffed her family claim, she says to the waiters, ''Do whatever he tells you.'' She gives priority to what Jesus wills, and so he goes ahead and performs the first of the signs that manifest his glory. In her own way, even though she has misunderstood and had her misunderstanding rejected, the fact that she has faith and stresses obedience to his word means that her request becomes the occasion of the first of Jesus' signs which causes his disciples to believe in him.

That John intends her to be seen in a positive light is confirmed by the later scene where John brings the mother of Jesus to the foot of the cross (19:25–27). That scenario constitutes a radical departure from the common tradition of the other Gospels. There Jesus is alone on the cross surrounded by the two bandits; at the foot of the cross stand only hostile figures who mock him; the women stand at a distance; and the male disciples are not presented at all. But in the Gospel according to John there are four people at the foot of the cross, of whom the most prominent are the mother of Jesus and the beloved disciple, two figures whose personal names are never given. (Yes, if we had only the Fourth Gospel, we would never have known the name of the mother of Jesus.) These two people are historical, but John is interested in them for symbolic reasons. The beloved disciple, whom John's community venerated more than any

other disciple of Jesus (even Peter the leader of the Twelve), is left name-
less because he is to serve as a model for all those whom Jesus loves.
Presumably the mother of Jesus also had a special symbolic significance
for the Johannine community. In any case the language of the scene at
the foot of the cross raises the issue of family relationship: "Woman,
behold your son. [Son] behold your mother." John comes to the basic
issue that the first three evangelists treated in their sole Marian scene:
Who constitute the mother and brother(s) of Jesus? The woman is not
simply the (physical) mother of Jesus; the role given her at the cross is
to be mother of the most beloved disciple. The Fourth Gospel treats
harshly the (physical) relatives called "the brothers of Jesus," who
never believed in him (7:5). It is rather the disciple whom he loves, who
now has Jesus' mother as his mother, who becomes the true brother of
Jesus. So on the cross John gives an answer to "Who are my mother and
my brothers" by pointing to the two who stand at the foot of the cross
and believe in Jesus. He leaves them behind as the family of disciples
who constitute truly a mother and a brother.

Although quite different from the other Gospels, John thus moves
in the same direction as Luke. These two evangelists know of Jesus'
"de-emphasis" of natural family that is so strong in the tradition. Yet,
as they face the reality of Mary, they recognize that, while she was natural family, she was part of the family of believers and even had a preeminent place in it. First Christian for Luke and mother of the ideal disciple
for John, she is true family for Jesus, not simply because of physical
relationship but because she meets the criterion of the gospel.

EXAMPLES OF BENEFITS:
ECUMENISM, POPULAR MARIAN DEVOTIONS

This NT trajectory, a line of development which becomes visible
in different ways in Luke and John, explains later Christian development. As we approach Mary ecumenically today, there arises an issue
of the validity of subsequent mariology. The wrong question (the one
unfortunately almost unfailingly posed by the very literal-minded and
conservative) is: Are the Marian doctrines found in the NT? Liberal
Catholics and many non-Catholics will answer negatively, with the implication that mariology should be rejected. This forces others to try to

prove that the Marian doctrines are in the NT. As I stressed in Chapter 2, however, part of the genius of Catholicism is that it does not confine itself to the limited insight of the first century (attested in the NT) but sees that tradition has continued to grow in a believing community of other centuries. In beginning the present chapter, I reported that a goal of *MNT* was to contribute to a probe of the relationship between the scriptural picture of Mary and the papally-defined dogmas of the Immaculate Conception and the Assumption. I argued on pp. 43-45 above that one cannot find these two doctrines in the NT, and this certainly was the direction of *MNT* as well. But that conclusion does not negate the raising of a more pertinent ecumenical issue: Are such Marian doctrines along lines of development that proceed from the NT? Critical exegesis uncovered a NT trajectory increasingly portraying Mary as a preeminent, and even the first, Christian disciple. Since deliverance from original sin and being raised from the dead to glory with Christ are privileges of Christian discipleship, Mary's role in being the first to enjoy these privileges[78] can be seen as a further development of the NT trajectory of priority in discipleship. True, at the present moment in ecumenism, most Protestants might not see this further development of mariology as a *necessary* direction of the trajectory of discipleship; but the type of historical-critical exegesis employed by ecumenical scholars in *MNT* should help many to see it as a *possible* direction from the NT. That is an extremely important gain, for no church union is possible when one party looks on the dogmas of the other as contradictory or completely foreign to the revelation attested by the inspired Scriptures.

A further growth in seeing the Marian dogmas not simply as a possible development in the NT trajectory of preeminent discipleship, but as a divinely guided development, will not come from scholarship, either exegetical or theological. It may come when Christians of different backgrounds live more closely together ecclesiastically, beginning to share one another's prayer life and intuitively perceiving each other's spiritual values. The Immaculate Conception and the Assumption made sense as divinely revealed dogmas to Roman Catholics when they were officially promulgated by popes because Catholics had a long liturgical life in

---

[78]See footnote 43 above for an understanding of the Assumption which involves resurrection from the dead.

which these doctrines were related to God's plan of salvation in Jesus Christ. That liturgical context should not be forgotten in discussions about whether other Christians can see the value of these dogmas.

These last remarks lead to another aspect of Mary's role in Roman Catholic life, namely, the popular national devotions to Mary often related to shrines or appearances: our Lady of Lourdes, of Czestochowa, of Guadalupe, etc. Liberal Catholic theologians have too often dismissed these devotions as irrelevant to solid Marian doctrine (not recognizing that symbols may be more revealing about the heart or core of a doctrine than are abstract statements), and non-Catholics have often been sore troubled to relate such devotions to biblical religion. Nevertheless, Catholic nations and peoples have sometimes found survival in clinging stubbornly to such devotions, so that the respective "Lady" has become a symbol of identity. If I may take our Lady of Guadalupe as an example, the exact details of the original vision that came so soon after the conquest of the New World are not easy to uncover,[79] but it is clear that this devotion to Mary was an intrinsic part of the acceptance of the Christian gospel by Mexican Indians. The Mary of Guadalupe was portrayed in the ancient garb of the mother of the deities whom the Indians had worshiped before Christianity. Thus the Indians were able to see that not all that had previously served them as religion had to be rejected: there was continuity between the old and the new. (Why should we think this insignificant when the NT shows us how important it was for the first Jews who accepted the gospel to insist to themselves and others that the Father of Jesus was truly the God of Abraham, of Isaac, and of Jacob, and that Jesus himself was consonant with the Law and the Prophets?) The Mexican Indians were reduced to slavery by conquerors who also proclaimed the gospel, a gospel that could easily have been understood by the forced converts in terms of might and power. But the Mary figure embodied the crucial message of love, compassion, and hope for the oppressed, making it possible to grasp what Jesus himself had proclaimed.

By way of concluding this chapter, let me relate this aspect of our Lady of Guadalupe to the Lucan scenes containing the annunciation and the *Magnificat*—scenes that in my earlier analysis of Mary in Luke I

---

[79]Not only are the ancient records in disagreement, but the preserved image of our Lady of Guadalupe is hard to analyze scientifically.

passed over quickly with the promise of later treatment. The angel's message to Mary about Jesus (1:31–35) identifies him as Son of David, Son of God; but then she goes forth and explains her interpretation of it in a hymn, the *Magnificat*. She does not proclaim the good news by saying that the Son of David and the Son of God is here. Rather, her soul magnifies the Lord and her spirit rejoices in God her savior because He has regarded the low estate of His *slave* woman. (We translate the word more politely as "handmaiden," but Mary speaks of the female slave. In the stratified society of the Roman Empire, slaves were among the lowest. When Pliny, the Roman governor, went looking for Christians to find out who this strange group was, he turned to slave women because among such creatures one would find Christians.) For Mary, the news about Jesus means that God has looked on the lowliness of a slave and, therefore, all generations would call her blessed. She has interpreted the christology in terms of what it means in the lives of people. God has put down the mighty and He has exalted the lowly. He has filled the hungry, and He has sent the rich away empty. He has helped His servant Israel in remembrance of His mercy.

This remarkable translation of what Son of David, Son of God mean is the same translation that Jesus the Son of David and the Son of God will himself make. In Luke 6:20–26 Jesus does not come proclaiming "I am Son of God." He says: Blessed are you who are poor, blessed are you who are hungry, and blessed are you who are persecuted; woe to you who are rich, woe to you who have enough, and woe to you when you are content. The gospel of God's Son means salvation for those who have nothing. That is the way Jesus translates it and that is the way Mary translates it. It is not without accident that the people today who characterize this as a radical mariology often see no connection between orthodox christology and social concern. They not only criticize modern theologians; they also criticize the bishops of the church when they say anything for the poor and the oppressed. Such critics are willing to believe the good news that Jesus is the Son of God provided that it not be translated into economic terms for the poor and the downtrodden.

Luke presents Mary as a disciple not only because she said, "Be it done unto me according to your word," but because she understood what that word meant in terms of the life of the poor and the slaves of whom she was a representative. And I think that is exactly what happened in the case of our Lady of Guadalupe. She gave the hope of the gospel to a whole people who had no other reason to see good news in what came from Spain. In their lives the devotion to our Lady constituted an authentic development of the gospel of discipleship.

So both on the ecumenical level and in terms of popular devotion, I think that modern insight into the Scriptures is very productive and loyal to the best traditions of mariology. One of the most perceptive Marian statements that Pope Paul VI ever made was contained in perhaps the last significant document he wrote about her (*Marialis Cultus,* Feb. 1974). I could not phrase better the result of modern biblical criticism in relation to Mary:

> The Virgin Mary has always been proposed to the faithful by the Church as an example to be imitated, not precisely in the type of life she led, and much less for the socio-cultural background in which she lived and which today scarcely exists anywhere.

We know so little about Mary historically that the exact village circumstances of her life cannot be duplicated. That is not the way we imitate Mary. And those that think they can conjecture about her life by imagination and historicize it do not understand why the church has proposed Mary to be imitated. The Pope says there is another way:

> Rather she is held up as an example to the faithful for the way in which in her own particular life she fully and responsibly accepted the will of God, because she heard the word of God and did it, and because charity and the spirit of service were the driving force of her actions. She is worthy of imitation because she was the first and most perfect of Christ's disciples.

Chapter 6
DIVERSE VIEWS OF THE SPIRIT IN THE NEW TESTAMENT— A PRELIMINARY CONTRIBUTION OF EXEGESIS TO DOCTRINAL REFLECTION

One could fill a whole library section with Catholic publications on Mary in the NT. But current exegesis has not been equally intensive about all issues, and in my judgment there is no truly adequate book on the Spirit in the NT exploring all pertinent texts in a critical, modern way. There is a new book on Christ in the NT almost every year, but there is an almost total absence of *comprehensive* books on the Spirit in the NT.[80] I pointed out in Chapter 1 that, according to some adversaries, historical criticism overly dominates contemporary exegesis. I supply this chapter to help readers grasp how much *more* critical exegesis has to be done on significant topics—the problem is not of too much, but of too little on the right issues.

A discussion of the Holy Spirit deals with a very challenging, and in a way, a very perplexing topic. There are some people in this world who do not believe in the God whom we call Father. There are many

---

[80]In this treatment I have found very helpful G. S. Hendry, *The Holy Spirit in Christian Theology* (rev. ed.; Philadelphia: Westminster, 1965). Useful books include: C. K. Barrett, *The Holy Spirit and the Gospel Tradition* (New York: Macmillan, 1947); J. D. G. Dunn, *Jesus and the Spirit* (London: SCM, 1975); H. Gunkel, *The Influence of the Holy Spirit* (Philadelphia: Fortress, 1979; German orig. 1888); G. T. Montague, *The Holy Spirit: Growth of a Biblical Tradition* (New York: Paulist, 1976); E. Schweizer, *The Holy Spirit* (Philadelphia: Fortress, 1980).

people who do not believe in God's Son, Jesus Christ. But it is very hard to determine how many there are who do not believe in the Holy Spirit. For some, perhaps, the Holy Spirit is not important enough to make a decision about; for other people, simpler and more primitive, the reality of the Spirit of God is so self-evident that they would not dare to question it. And yet that very silence about the Holy Spirit reflects our problem. Although the Spirit is attested by the Scriptures, Old and New, it remains mysterious and vague. Even when we turn to the Creeds for enlightenment, the *Apostles Creed,* which expatiates about the Father and the Son, says simply "I believe in the Holy Spirit," without explaining what the Spirit does. In the longer *Creed of Nicaea,* enlarged by Constantinople (the Creed of 381, of which we recently celebrated the 1500th anniversary), there is this information about the Holy Spirit: "We believe in the Holy Spirit, the Lord and Giver of life, who proceeds from the Father, who together with the Father and the Son is adored and glorified, who spoke by the prophets." Startlingly, most of that is OT information: the Holy Spirit has come forth from God; he is to be glorified; and he spoke through the prophets. But what did the Spirit do in relation to Jesus Christ in Christian history? The Creed does not tell us.

As a result of the silence one may argue with permissible exaggeration that this one Spirit whom we praise ("one Lord, one Spirit, one baptism") has been the most divisive feature in the history of Christianity. In the great Councils of the first millennium of Christianity the churches could agree on God and (for the most part) on Jesus Christ; but East and West ultimately split apart over the Spirit. The West adhered to the notion that the Spirit comes forth from the Son (*filioque*) as well as from the Father, a view rejected by the East as an intrusion in the Christian creedal faith. For the East the Spirit proceeds from the Father alone.

And if in the first millennium the relation of the Spirit to Christ divided Eastern Christianity from Western, in the mid-second millennium the relation of the Spirit to the church subdivided the West. The Reformation was a battle among Western Christians who were united in the belief that the Spirit had come forth from the Son (as well as from the Father) but who were very divided over how the Spirit functioned in the church. Did he function in such a way that the official spokesmen of the church, the hierarchy or bishops, were the interpreters of the Christian faith? Or could the Spirit speak through the Scriptures in such a way that readers of the Scriptures could challenge the teachings of the church hierarchy? If the answer to those questions divided Western Christianity into Protestant and Roman Catholic, Protestant Christianity can be said to have divided further on whether that Spirit speaks through the Scriptures *in the church* (as both Calvin and Luther would insist) or so *individually* in the heart of every Christian that the Bible read in a personal way, without church tradition or church setting, is an adequate guide. If I may oversimplify, the latter principle produced the charismatics and enthusiasts of "the Left Wing" of the Reformation.

Moving on from the mid-second millennium, one may say that the 20th century is further divided on the problem of the Spirit of God and the human spirit. A real issue that faces Christianity today is whether we are to think simply of a vitalization of a human spirit that is already in every man and woman by the fact of existence on this earth, or still to believe in a Spirit given by God that goes beyond our own potentialities, the Spirit of a revealing and endowing God.

Even the biblical situation is complex, for the term "spirit" is ambiguous. The Greek word *pneuma* occurs about 380 times in the NT. Many times it refers to evil spirits, angelic spirits, or simply and vaguely "spirits." Rather seldom does *pneuma* clearly refer to what we know as the Holy Spirit. When one presses back to the Master, the term "Holy Spirit" or "the Spirit" in this proper sense occurs relatively seldom on Jesus' lips. (Yet for him the Spirit is not insignificant: blasphemy against the Son of Man can be forgiven, but not blasphemy against the Holy Spirit—a harsh warning.) *Pneuma* occurs some 70 times in the Book of Acts, almost one-fifth of the NT instances. The Book of Acts is the story of the church; and so we may deduce that, drawing from the relatively few instances in Jesus' own discourse, the church gave *pneuma* a major role. Also in the Pauline Letters, the elevation of the Spirit is startling. Already in the opening five verses of I Thessalonians, the first extant Christian writing composed about A.D. 50 when Christianity was not twenty years old, we hear of God the Father, the Lord Jesus Christ, and *the Spirit*. The famous blessing at the end of II Corinthians (13:13) involves the grace of the Lord Jesus Christ, and the love of God, and the fellowship of the Holy Spirit. In the divided Corinthian church there are varieties of gifts but the same Spirit; varieties of service, but the same Lord; and varieties of workings but the same God (I Cor 12:4–6). It is very clear that God the Father, the Lord Jesus Christ, and the Spirit are already on a level within the first 20 years of the Christian message. But on that level, how do they function?

The Father, God, is *Kyrios*, "Lord," a name used in Greek to render the YAHWEH of the Israelite Scriptures. Jesus also is *Kyrios*, "Lord," for he is given the name that is above every other name (Phil 2:9). Finally there is that solemn statement in II Cor 3:17 "The Lord is the Spirit; where the Spirit of the Lord is, there is freedom." Thus the same divine name is used of all three; yet the same things are not affirmed of all three. Jesus says "The Father is greater than I," and the Spirit is the Spirit of Jesus Christ.

Granted this unity and disunity, let me now try to organize the NT material under the three divisions I discussed in my opening remarks: the Spirit and Christ; the Spirit and the church; and the Spirit and humanity.

THE SPIRIT AND CHRIST

The NT reflection on the Spirit was part of the Christian attempt to understand Jesus. Despite the crucifixion, belief gained through an encounter with the risen Jesus forced Christians to say that he was the fulfillment of the OT promises, even though many of those promises had not been fulfilled visibly. Christians sought to detect such fulfillment in the various moments of Jesus' life.

Very clearly the resurrection early served this purpose: Jesus had been among them as a servant, but then God had elevated him and exalted him through the resurrection. Connected with that was the gift of the Spirit. In part, this connection may have been made because "spirit" was the life-giving power. In early Hebrew understanding, "spirit" and "breath" are one word, so that God gave to human beings the spirit of life. In Gen 7:21–22 all flesh consists of "all in whose nostrils is the spirit of life." "The Lord stretches out the heavens," says Zechariah (12:1), "and forms the spirit of a human being within him." When one is alive, then, one has the spirit. When one dies, one gives up the spirit, as Jesus did on the cross when he breathed out his Spirit. And what God did in the resurrection was to return the Spirit to Jesus; and in this returning of the Holy Spirit, Jesus is glorified. We hear of this glorification in old creedal formulas in the NT, some of them in the Pauline writings but possibly antedating Paul, e.g., "Jesus was vindicated *in the Spirit*"

(I Tim 3:16). Famous is the passage in Romans 1:3–4 about Jesus, God's Son, who was descended from David according to the flesh, but constituted Son of God in power *through the Holy Spirit* (literally, Spirit of Holiness) by resurrection from the dead. What an awesome conglomeration of ideas: God constituted Jesus as His Son through the Holy Spirit in power by resurrection. This connection of the Spirit with resurrection was so vivid in Christian minds because their encounter with the risen Jesus brought them the same kind of power that marked Jesus' ministry, as we shall see when we turn to the theme of Spirit and the church.

Still, the resurrection context is not adequate to understand the role of the Spirit. If one associates the Spirit with the resurrection, how was the Spirit in Jesus during his life and his ministry? There is a very strange statement in the Fourth Gospel that may catch Christian reflection on this problem. In John 7:39 Jesus speaks by way of promise: from within him (presumably from himself) there shall flow rivers of living water. The evangelist attempts to enlighten us: by the "living water" Jesus was referring to the Spirit which those who came to believe in him were to receive, "For as yet there was no Spirit." Usually this peculiar statement is translated, "For as yet the Spirit had not been given"; but that is not what the author writes. He writes, "As yet there was no Spirit," almost as if the Spirit as a reality for Christians would not come into effect until after the ministry of Jesus.

Yet other NT passages insist very strongly that the Spirit was present in the ministry of Jesus, whether it could be recognized by his followers or not. In the Lucan reference (11:20) to the healings and, especially, to the driving out of demons, Jesus says "If it is by the *finger of God* that I cast out demons, then the kingdom of God has come upon you." But Matthew (12:28) writes, "If it is *by the Holy Spirit* that I cast out demons then the kingdom of God has come upon you." This changed wording means that as Christians reflected on Jesus' language during his ministry when he characterized divine assistance as the finger of God, they saw that assistance embodied in the Holy Spirit. All the Gospels, at the very beginning of Jesus' public ministry, connect his identity with the Holy Spirit coming down upon him at his baptism. In the Pauline formulas we heard that Jesus was constituted Son of God through the Holy Spirit by resurrection from the dead. But in the Gospels, as declared by God himself, Jesus is God's Son through the Holy Spirit by baptism. And Luke 4:14 says, "He returned to Galilee in the *power* of

Chapter 6

the Spirit," still using language similar to Romans. In the Spirit the power of God came upon him; and, indeed, in Luke 4:16–18, when Jesus opens the Scriptures in his first sermon, he begins: "The Spirit of the Lord is upon me."

The full Christian understanding of Jesus as possessing the Holy Spirit is not satisfied by resorting to the beginning of the ministry. It is not sufficient to say that through the resurrection Jesus is Son of God through the Holy Spirit; it is not sufficient to say that through the baptism Jesus is Son of God through the Holy Spirit. Reaching back earlier, Matthew and Luke start their Gospels with *the conception* of Jesus through the Holy Spirit. Indeed, the angel Gabriel in Luke 1:35 virtually recites for Mary what Paul recites as a Christian creed. If Paul writes, "constituted Son of God in power through the Holy Spirit by resurrection," Gabriel changes resurrection to conception and says to Mary, "The *Holy Spirit* will come upon you; the *power* of the Most High will overshadow you; therefore the child will be called holy, the *Son of God*." The sense that the Holy Spirit was an integral part of Jesus' identity has been applied to his conception.

Even this perception is not adequate in the Christian struggle to understand Christ and the Spirit, for others will implicitly identify the Spirit that comes on Jesus Christ with the Spirit of God that moved across the waters at the creative moment (Gen 1:2). The creator Spirit is seen to be part of the mystery of Christ. And so John does not begin his story of Jesus Christ with either the baptism or the conception of Jesus. He moves the Jesus story back to the creation: "In the beginning was the Word, and the Word was with God. The Word was God. . . . Through him all things came into being" (John 1:1–2). John echoes the beginning of Genesis when the Spirit moved over the waters while God spoke the creative word. One psalm (104:30) says "You send forth Your spirit and they are created"; another Psalm (148:5) says God "*commanded* and they were created." The Word of God and His Spirit were both involved in the creation, and they were together from the beginning.

THE SPIRIT AND THE CHURCH

In all these stages (creation, conception, baptism, resurrection) the Spirit plays a role in what God has done in Jesus Christ, so intimate a role that one cannot separate the two. Jesus acts by the Spirit: if the Spirit creates, the Word creates; if the Spirit sanctifies, Jesus sanctifies. That same understanding is carried over as the church reflects on itself, but now the Spirit succeeds to Jesus. He is the last actor in the divine plan that began with creation and has continued with the cross and resurrection. In various works of the NT, however, there are different views of how the Spirit works in the Christian community, in the church.

In the 50s at Corinth, Paul sees many roles and activities in the church: there are apostles and prophets and teachers and healers—such a variety of gifts, but the same Spirit. Or even, there are Spirits, for Paul uses the plural: "Being zealous for the Spirits, seek for the edification of the church" (I Cor 14:12). The Spirit is a many-splendored thing, so that it breaks up into manifestations. A special gift of the Spirit is required in order to discern the Spirits. This view would have the Spirit endow Christians with abilities. Yet there are ambiguities in this concept. Clearly, Paul would say that he was not an apostle because of any ability of his own—that was a gift directly from God. One might speak similarly of the prophet and the healer. But would Paul say the same for the teacher and administrator? Do those functions involve the gift of the Holy Spirit working *with the human spirit*? To what extent is such a gift or such a spirit both from above and below at the same time? We never get information on that. The very fact that people want a specific gift of the Spirit not already possessed means that in some way the Spirit corresponds to the human personality. Paul's description of the gifts of the spirits or charisms at Corinth is a favorable description. (He himself has the gift of apostleship, speaks in tongues, and can prophesy.) Yet he is also aware of the divisive nature of such gifts or spirits in the Christian community. Paul insists that it is just as foolish for someone who has one gift to want another as for the hand to want to be a foot. His whole imagery of the one body of Christ is sketched because the gifts of the Spirit are also a dividing factor.

We see in the later derivatives of Pauline theology how ultimately that factor became too divisive, so that another understanding of the Spirit developed. In Timothy and Titus, the letters called Pastoral, where Paul is disappearing from the scene, the question arises: How is the church of the future to be provided for when there are no more apostles? The answer is to choose the presbyter-bishops (and deacons), i.e., church administrators, and get them in place in every church. They can preserve the tradition; church office will hold the church together. And it is understood that when a church officer is selected, the Holy Spirit is involved in empowering that office. (This correlation of office and Spirit becomes even more rigid in subsequent church writings.) Instead of the Spirit spontaneously endowing various members within the community, the Spirit is seen to function much more in the organized structure of the church, particularly in the ability of the presbyter-bishops to teach. In the language of sociology, there is a routinization of the Spirit. Such a Spirit-endowed structure has a great advantage—it will continue. Charismatic groups are always imperiled if the charism does not reappear in the second generation. The great charismatic leaders of Israel, the Judges, were finally left by the wayside because in moments of real need there might be no one who had a charism. The monarchy was established with the claim that the Spirit of wisdom and understanding came on the king at the moment of his coronation; and so the Spirit was tied to the royal institution in the guidance of God's people. The same thing happened in the Christian community. In place of many diverse charisms, the Spirit functioned more surely through the office.

But such routinization is not a total picture. The Book of Acts, which is related to the Pauline tradition in some way, emphasizes another understanding of the Spirit. Acts thinks of the Spirit coming like a mighty wind at Pentecost when the disciples do not know what to do, even though they have seen the risen Lord. It is the Spirit that drives them to preach, indicating that their task is to proclaim Jesus Christ. Later on, the apostles stay on in Jerusalem and are not pictured as quickly moving out; but the Spirit drives other Christian missionaries from Jerusalem to approach outsiders—Samaritans and eventually even Gentiles. Peter, the leader of the Twelve Apostles, is totally astounded; but if the Spirit wills to be poured forth on even the Gentiles, why should Peter resist (Acts 10:46)? When the ultimate decision destined to shape the whole nature of Christianity comes up in the so-called Council of Jerusalem, namely, the question whether the church is to be open freely and totally to the Gentiles, it is settled thus: "It has seemed good to the Holy Spirit and to us" (Acts 15:28). In other words, Acts does not emphasize a Spirit attached to office, but a Spirit that comes sweeping in at decisive moments to tell the apostolic figures what to do. If one may use stage language in a way that is not pejorative, we have a *Deus ex machina,* with the Spirit of God coming in to solve the issue.

Such a Spirit has remained a very strong anticipation in Christian thought. In great moments the Spirit acts in the church in some undefinable way and moves the church towards what it should do. At the opening of the Second Vatican Council there was a solemn prayer to the Spirit because this was looked on as a moment when the church uniquely needed guidance. As a matter of fact, at the Council the Spirit led the church in a different way from what many church officials wanted and expected—even though in Catholic theology those officers received that Spirit when they received their office. In other words we had a modern example of the Spirit-endowed office of the Pastoral Epistles being corrected by the occasionally on-rushing Spirit of the Book of Acts. Another problem is that Acts, with its thesis of the Spirit arriving at chosen moments, tends to give a blank check on the Spirit. We Christians can always claim that we have done what we have done because the Spirit led us. But it is not so easy to prove the Spirit's influence. There is a story told of an elderly Roman Catholic woman who was quite resistant to all the changes of Vatican II. She fought her pastor all the time. Finally he lost his patience with her and said: "Can't you see that the Holy Spirit is leading the church to make all these changes?" And she answered him, "Well, that's funny; the Holy Spirit is leading us to make changes that the Holy Ghost never used to approve of!" In other words, when the church depends on the overall guidance of the Holy Spirit and then makes radical changes, do such changes imply that the Spirit was not with the church's practice previously?

There is still another powerful understanding of the relation between the Spirit and the church that is not covered by charisms (I Corinthians), by Spirit-endowed office (Pastorals), or by the great moving Spirit (Acts). It is found in the Gospel of John. That Gospel developed another term for the Spirit, not the neuter term *pneuma* but *paraklētos*, a personal term.[81] "Paraclete" defies definition. It is a legal term, "advocate," and certainly the Johannine Spirit has legal functions in defending Jesus Christ and proclaiming the world wrong. The ultimate proof that Jesus was victorious over death is that a personal Spirit who represents him testifies. In the OT, Job ultimately realized he could not prove himself right in the trial before God; but he prayed that his vin-

[81]The second volume of my Anchor Bible commentary on the Gospel according to John (Garden City, NY: Doubleday, 1970)1136–44 gives a detailed treatment of the concept of the Paraclete and a bibliography on this difficult subject.

dicating angel would stand upon his grave and prove to the world that he was right (Job 19:25). Similarly, the Paraclete, the Spirit of Truth, is the defending angel of Christ. He is also the teacher of the individual Christian: "If you love me and keep my commandments, then at my request the Father will give you another Paraclete to be with you forever" (14:15). "The Paraclete, the Holy Spirit . . . will teach you everything" (14:26). Thus the Spirit is not confined to charismatics, whether they be apostles or prophets or teachers or administrators, but is the possession of every believing Christian. The ultimate teacher of the church is not the property of any office. The church was not crippled when the apostles died; for, indeed, it was the Paraclete/Spirit that enabled the first generation to bear witness. This same Paraclete/Spirit enables the ordinary believer to bear witness just as effectively as the first generation bore witness. This is not the sweeping Spirit of Acts, coming at an awesome moment; rather, the Paraclete is always there. Ultimately such an understanding of the Spirit means that there is no such thing as a second-class Christian either in position or in time because every Christian has the Spirit of God in his or her heart. And yet, this understanding too has its difficulties. If the Spirit is in the heart of every Christian, what happens when two Christians disagree? How do people know which is the voice of the Spirit? Later on in this same Johannine tradition that gave us the Paraclete, another writer has to warn complainingly, "Do not believe every Spirit; rather put these Spirits to the test . . . so we can know the Spirit of Truth from the Spirit of Deceit" (I John 4:1, 6).

THE SPIRIT AND THE HUMAN SPIRIT

We turn to the final question, after our discussions of the Spirit and Christ and of the Spirit and the church. What about the Spirit and the human spirit? If there is the Spirit of Truth that comes from God, and if according to the NT there is a Spirit of Deceit that comes from the devil, we can say further that there is the human spirit. It is neither precisely of God nor of the devil; but unfortunately it is capable of working not only with God but also with evil. There the Scriptures show ambiguity. God created us by breathing into us a living spirit, and so every living human being has the spirit. When God gives us life, He answers the prayer, "Send forth Your spirit." Job (34:14–15) cries out, "When God takes back His spirit . . . human beings descend into the dust." Still the OT insists that there is a special spirit. Every human being may have from God the life-giving spirit; but when the Spirit comes on Elijah, he can act as a prophet. He passes on a two-fold Spirit to Elisha, and that person becomes different—a prophet more mighty in deeds than his master. Every human being may have the spirit, but the king at his coronation gets the Spirit of wisdom and understanding and counsel and fortitude and knowledge and piety or fear of the Lord (Isa 11:2). Every human being may have the life-giving spirit; but when Saul in an unforgettable moment is seized by the "Spirit of God," that king of Israel rolls about naked in the dust and everyone says: "Is Saul also among the prophets?" (I Sam 19:23–24). Evidently biblical writers could distinguish between the human spirit that comes from God and a special Spirit that comes from God. The same distinction is true in the NT. All human beings are created in God's image and likeness, and thus all have His spirit. Yet, according to Paul and to John, those who believe in Jesus Christ receive God's Holy Spirit. They are the children of God! As uncomfortable and exclusive as it may seem, one would be hard pressed to find either John or Paul saying that every human being is a child of God. Childhood or sonship is the particular privilege of whose who are given the Spirit of Jesus Christ.

What difference does Jesus Christ make in the special Spirit given in his name? Eastern and Western Christianity are divided over that point. If we identify the Redeemer's Spirit with the creator Spirit, that creator Spirit proceeds from the Father. Yet does not Jesus Christ, the Redeemer, make a difference? God never changes; but in trinitarian life God the Son becomes human, and he was not human before. Classical theologians cannot admit change, and so they posit only a new relationship in God. Yet because the Son of God lived as we live, and died even more horribly than most of us die, is not God's experience different? Therefore, when the Spirit is given by Jesus Christ, is not that Spirit marked by the Son as well as by the Father? The Spirit that lives in the hearts of those who are God's children, conformed to the image of Jesus Christ—is it not different in some way from the spirit that conforms all human beings to the creator God? In another way of asking the question, can we be satisfied with saying that all that is noble comes forth from the human spirit that exists within us? Ultimately, must we not turn to God's Spirit who comes into us and not simply out of us?

*   *   *

I have said that in the Bible "spirit" has many meanings; often diverse meanings receive the same treatment in modern thought. As part of demythologization, the devil as the evil spirit is lost to many Christians. Inevitably, then, the spirit as the Holy Spirit of God is going to be lost. The same mentality which claims that in the world there can be no evil which is not of our creation will ultimately say that in the world there can be no good which is not of our creation. The mystery of evil, however we express it, is closely tied to the mystery of good. It is interesting to reflect on hell as an embodiment of the mystery of evil. Among some strands of modern thought one may find parallels to ideas expressed in such diverse writers as Milton and Jean-Paul Sartre. According to Milton's Satan, "Hell is myself"; and indeed many could say, "I myself constitute my own hell." According to one of Sartre's characters, "Hell is other people"; and, alas, in the complex issues of life, including those of the family, our hell often is other people. But the classical definition of hell is the absence of God; and experiencing the absence of God may still be the most profound understanding of what it is for a human being to go through hell. The Holy Spirit is the refutation of that hell.

God was diffusive of His being in creating a good world that mirrored Him, and epecially in creating intelligent human beings that mirrored His intelligence. But God could not be satisfied until He became embroiled in human history with all its successes and failures by identifying Himself with one people. (Israel as the special people of God is a concept with the faults of particularism, but we can never live by abstractions.) Still God was not satisfied, and so He further embroiled Himself in one human life, that of Jesus Christ. But God's ultimate act of presence to the world that He created and redeemed involves His entrance into individual lives as the Holy Spirit. The Holy Spirit is the ultimate revelation of God. If hell is the final absence of God, the Spirit is the supreme presence of God—a presence that the Book of Acts describes as a mighty wind and tongues of fire, a presence that a Christian hymn describes as a sweet cooling (*dulce refrigerium*). The Spirit brings burning power and cooling consolation and whatever gift is needed to assure us of the truth of the promise of the Johannine Jesus: ''If you love me and keep my commandments the Father will give you another Paraclete, the Spirit of Truth, to be with you forever. . . . He remains with you and is within you'' (John 14:15–17).

This is not yet a trinitarian doctrine of the Spirit; but to many that doctrine will seem a meaningless abstraction unless it takes into account the NT factors (uncovered by a very inchoative exegesis) that I have described in this chapter.

Chapter 7
THE NEW TESTAMENT BACKGROUND FOR THE EMERGING DOCTRINE OF "LOCAL CHURCH"

The Reformation, faced with rejection by the large church centralized in the papacy, gave great stress to the local church. In 1530, a description of the church was given in the Augsburg Confession (7) as "the assembly of all believers among whom the gospel is preached in its purity and the holy sacraments are administered according to the gospel." The first part of this description ("the assembly of all believers") was somewhat neglected, and the worshiping community with preaching and sacrament was often identified simply as the church. By reaction Roman Catholicism before Vatican II placed its emphasis on the church universal. Without denying catholicity (universality), Vatican II gave rise to a renewed interest among Roman Catholics in the local church. It is interesting how a key statement of the Council[82] invoked the Scriptures on this issue: "This Church of Christ is truly present in all legitimate local congregations of the faithful which, united with their pastors, are themselves called churches in the New Testament."

The relation of the local church to the universal church (and in particular to Rome) is an emerging doctrine in Roman Catholicism, the future of which is still not clear. Many factors, some of them quite practical and ordinary, will contribute to the shaping of that doctrine, e.g., how

---

[82]*Lumen Gentium* (Dogmatic Constitution on the Church) 3.26; DVII 50.

much decisive authority does Rome allot to the National Episcopal Conferences or to local bishops; how much local liturgical expression and uniqueness does the pope tolerate in his journeys throughout the world; what regional sacramental practices are not forbidden. Critical exegesis of the NT will also make its contribution to the emerging doctrine.[83] A preliminary survey of some of those contributions may be drawn from these comments I made about local NT churches to a group of theologians who were studying the issue.[84]

REGIONAL CHURCHES AND "THE CHURCH"

In the past it has been almost an axiom of biblical scholarship that the term "church," *ekklēsia,* was used first for the Christian community of a given region or city before it was applied more abstractly to the whole body of Christians ("*the* church"). This opinion is based chiefly on Pauline usage, for in the Proto-Pauline Epistles[85] we find "the church of the Thessalonians" (I Thess 1:1), "the churches of Galatia" (Gal 1:1), "the church of God which is in Corinth" (I Cor 1:1; II Cor 1:1), "the churches of God which are in Judea" (I Thess 2:14). In some of the Deutero-Pauline Epistles we find a more generalized concept: "the church" is the body of Christ according to Col 1:18, while Eph 5:25 states that "Christ loved the church and gave himself up for her." Nevertheless, a wider range of evidence indicates *a more complex situation* than that suggested by the axiom "first particular, then general or universal."

(1) The Pauline usage itself is far from clear. A serious debate is still centered on whether Colossians might not be Proto-Pauline; and even if one sides with the majority of scholars in favor of the Deutero-Pauline judgment, the line of demarcation between the earlier Epistles and Colossians is not clear. The usage of "the church" in Colossians

---

[83]Even as I write this in April 1985, the Pontifical Biblical Commission is meeting in Rome to discuss the issue of local churches.

[84]The June 1981 36th Annual Convention of the Catholic Theological Society of America.

[85]I Thessalonians, Galatians, I–II Corinthians, Romans, Philippians and Philemon are the undisputed Pauline Epistles. "Deutero-Pauline" means that works may not be by Paul himself but are within the "Pauline school."

can be related to the usage in I Cor 12:28: "God has appointed in the church first apostles, second prophets, then teachers. . . ." It is almost impossible to think that in the Corinthian statement "the church" is the regional community of Corinth, for such figures as apostles, prophets, and teachers are attested in many churches of the NT period.[86] As Bultmann correctly observes in comment on I Cor 12:28, "By the person and the work of the apostles, prophets, and teachers the Ecclesia is represented as the *one* Church."[87] Indeed, the study of individual Pauline Epistles shows little precision in Paul's use of *ekklēsia* in terms of the one and the many. In Gal 1:13 he can speak of having persecuted "the church of God"[88] and in Gal 1:22 of not being known by sight "to the churches of Judea which are in Christ." If in I Cor 14:34 Paul says, "The women should keep silence in the churches," in the very next verse he says, "It is shameful for a woman to speak in church." And while he addresses "the church of God which is in Corinth" (I Cor 1:1), he speaks of "the churches of Galatia" (16:1) and "the churches of Asia" (16:19).

(2) If in the Pauline usage of *ekklēsia* there is no clear progression from the many to the one, neither is there precision in other works of the NT. The word appears in only one of the four Gospels, so that it is scarcely a common term in the Jesus tradition. In Matthew, a work of the 80s, we find the same general/particular ambiguity as in the Pauline Epistles of the 50s. The *ekklēsia* of Matt 16:18, "You are Peter and upon this rock I shall build my church," surely covers more than a regional community; yet the only other Matthean passage (18:17) just as surely refers to a local community, for the complaint against the recalcitrant brother (who will listen neither privately nor before several witnesses) is to be referred "to the church." Roughly contemporaneous with Matthew is Luke/Acts. While most of the uses of *ekklēsia* in Acts are for

---

[86]See Acts 13:1; Eph 2:20; 4:11.

[87]R. Bultmann, *Theology of the New Testament* (2 vols.; New York: Scribners, 1951, 1955) 2.104.

[88]It is not certain whether this expression (also I Cor 15:9) involves a generalized use of "church" or refers to "the church of God which is in Judea" (I Thess 2:14). L. Cerfaux, *The Church in the Theology of St. Paul* (New York: Herder and Herder, 1959) 106–14, favors the latter position, arguing that "the church of God" was originally a title used exclusively for the church of Jerusalem.

regional communities,[89] a more generalized usage is in Acts 9:31: "The church throughout all Judea, Galilee, and Samaria." The Johannine usage is uncertain. In the corpus of Gospel and Epistles *ekklēsia* occurs only in III John and there seemingly for a local community.[90] We do not know whether the Johannine writers would have used *ekklēsia* for the collectivity of Christians. Doubt is raised not only by Johannine silence but also by the hostility of the Johannine writers toward some who profess belief in Christ (John 6:60–65; 8:31ff.; 12:42–43; I John 2:19), and by the reference to "other sheep not of this fold" (John 10:16), so that unity is not yet attained but needs to be prayed for (17:21). In such an outlook could any one term describe an existing Christian universality? The cousin to the Johannine writings, the Book of Revelation (Apocalypse), knows of seven local churches in Asia Minor (1:11; 2:1, 8 etc.) but uses collective symbols for the Christian whole, such as the pregnant woman (12:4–5) and the Bride of the Lamb (19:7; 21:9).

(3) Clearer information about the relation between the churches and the church can be amassed if we move beyond the term *ekklēsia* to the self-understanding of the Christian community and to terms other than *ekklēsia*. The absence of *ekklēsia* from most of the Gospels and from the early chapters of Acts which describe the first Christian community before the beginning of the mission outside Jerusalem[91] suggests that only gradually did this term become the self-designation par excellence of the Christian community. The Semitic background is plausibly the usage of *qahal* ("assembly," LXX: *ekklēsia*) in the phrase "the church of the Lord" in Deut 23:1, to describe Israel in the desert. This would fit the self-conception of the earliest Christian community as the renewed Israel, symbolized by the Twelve who were to sit on (twelve)

---

[89]E.g., 8:1 for the church in Jerusalem, 13:1 in Antioch, 14:23 in Asia Minor, and 15:41 in Syria and Antioch.

[90]Clearly it refers to a regional church in III John 9, and probably also in III John 6. In II John 1 and 13 "Elect" (Lady) probably refers to a regional church, for the reasons explained in my Anchor Bible commentary on the Epistles (Garden City, NY: Doubleday, 1982) 651–55, 679–80.

[91]Before 8:1 (which marks the beginning of the mission outside Jerusalem) *ekklēsia* occurs only in 5:11 ("Great fear came upon the whole church [of Jerusalem]") and in 7:36 (a reference to the church of Israel in the desert—an important reference supporting the thesis to be mentioned about the background of the Christian term).

Chapter 7

thrones judging the twelve tribes of Israel (Matt 19:28; Luke 22:28–30). Let me suggest two other terms as candidates for earlier designations of the renewed Israel. In Acts 24:14[92] we find the term "the Way" (*hodos*, reflecting Hebrew *derek*) as Paul expresses his self-understanding in contrast to that of his Jewish opponents, "According to the Way, which they call a sect, I worship the God of our Fathers, believing everything laid down by the Law or written in the Prophets." The use of the term "the Way" in the Qumran self-description of the Dead Sea Scroll sectarians[93] makes plausible the thesis that Acts has preserved an early Jewish Christian self-designation of the community, which saw itself fulfilling the directive of God pertinent to Israel in Isa 40:3: "In the wilderness prepare the way of the Lord"—again a description of Israel in the desert on the way to the promised land (although this time in the exodus from Babylon rather than from Egypt). Notable too is the frequency of *koinōnia* in the NT to describe the participation, communion, or fellowship that holds Christians together,[94] for example, already in Acts 2:42 as a characteristic of the first Christian community in Jerusalem. It may be asked whether *koinōnia* does not have a Semitic antecedent in *yaḥad,* "community, oneness," which is once more a Dead Sea Scroll self-designation, for the basic rule book of the sectarians was entitled "The Book of the Ordinance of the *Yaḥad.*" Since the Dead Sea Scroll sectarians regarded themselves as the renewed Israel, these parallels confirm the thesis that the initial Christian self-understanding was in terms of Israel, and thus there was a sense of oneness or unity from the beginning. Acts 6–8 indicates that increase in numbers, disagreements, and a mission outside Jerusalem produced by persecution led to the development of diverse Christian communities and regional communities (see pp. 130-34 below). Paul's use of "the church of God" for

---

[92]Other special uses of "the Way" as a title for Christianity may be found in Acts 9:2; 19:9,23; 22:4; 24:22 (see also 16:17; 18:25–26).

[93]In the Community Rule (1QS 8:12–14) we read: "When these people join the Community [*yaḥad*] in Israel, according to these rules they shall separate from the habitation of wicked men to go into the wilderness to prepare the way of God, as it is written [Isa 40:3]. . . ."

[94]While in itself the word *koinōnia* can describe the concrete results of communion, namely "community," the NT usage favors the spirit of communion that produces community. See Schuyler Brown, "Koinonia as the Basis of New Testament Ecclesiology?" *One in Christ* 12 (1976), 157–67.

such regional communities indicates that they were to see themselves as patterned upon and imitative of the church in Judea. The universal sense of "the church" would preserve (or regain) the original unity. Thus, in tracing how Christians understood themselves as a church, one could argue for a logical progression from original unity to regional or ideological diversity and finally to universality. Any thesis that would give priority to the local or regional church runs up against the indication in Acts that at one time the local community of Jerusalem was the whole church.[95]

HOUSE CHURCHES OF THE PAULINE MISSION

There is ambiguity in our own, contemporary use of the term "local church." For instance, does the term refer to the Roman Catholic Church in a country, as distinct from other countries, or to the diocesan church under the bishop, or to the parish church as the smallest unit? A similar question must be raised when we begin considering regional churches in the NT era. If Paul speaks of "the churches of Galatia" or "the churches of Asia" (I Cor 16:1,19), his plural may cover the church in each city or town in Galatia and Asia, so that the smallest unit would be comparable to "the church of God which is in Corinth" (I Cor 1:2). However, as Christianity grew, we know of a smaller unit, exemplified by plural house churches in the same city. If we wish to consider local churches in the NT period, we must deal with house churches; and I shall begin with the simplest form of this phenomenon, the house churches of the Pauline mission. I speak of "simplest form" for several reasons. The pattern of Paul's mission meant that most often he was the first Christian missionary to come into an area (I Cor 3:10–15; Rom 15:20: he did not build on another man's foundation); and so at least for a while all the churches in a Pauline city would have stemmed from the same mission. Moreover, it is Paul who gives us the most information about the exis-

---

[95]Caution is necessary, however, for Acts 18:24–19:7 describes Christians at Ephesus (some of them coming from Alexandria) as late as A.D. 55 who knew nothing of Christian baptism or of the Holy Spirit. Such a group could scarcely have had their origins in the Jerusalem community described at Pentecost which made the Holy Spirit and baptism part of the fundamental instruction (2:38). Plausibly such a group could have derived from early followers of Jesus during the public ministry who had no further contact with the mainline group of followers symbolized by the Twelve.

tence of house churches.[96] Let me sample a few of the questions that a study of the Pauline house church might raise for theology.
(1) *Church structure.* In his earliest preserved letter (I Thess 5:12) Paul speaks of "those who are over you in the Lord and admonish you." In the list of charisms in I Cor 12:28 Paul mentions the charism of administration (*kybernēsis*). In Philip 1:1 he sends greetings "to the bishops and the deacons."[97] And the Pastoral Epistles pay great attention to presbyters and deacons who must be appointed in every city (Titus 1:5) to govern the church in the aftermath of Paul's death. Thus, from one end of the Pauline corpus to the other, there are various figures of local authority. What relation to such authority was maintained by the owner of the house in which the respective church met? Were the householders eventually among those who were over the Thessalonians in the Lord? Were they among the bishops of Philippians and the presbyter-bishops of the Pastorals? (If not, there must have been some very sharp conflicts from time to time between householders and those charged with pastoral authority over the church meeting in the house.) It would seem that the householder had to have at least one form of authority since he had the power of the keys and could refuse admittance to his house. (The importance of this power is apparent in II John 10 where it is urged that false teachers not be received into the house [church], a power of refusal that III John 9 describes as being exercised by one who puts himself first in the church.) A connection between the householder and the presbyter is suggested by some of the family descriptions in the job description of the presbyters in the Pastorals: the presbyter must be married only once, one whose children are believers, able to manage his own house well and to keep his children in order (Titus 1:6; I Tim 3:4). The relations of

[96]Among the passages to be considered are Rom 16:5,14,15; I Cor 16:19; Philem 2; Col 4:15. Important treatments in English include F. V. Filson, "The Significance of the Early House Churches," *Journal of Biblical Literature* 58 (1939) 105–12; A. Malherbe, *Social Aspects of Early Christianity* (Baton Rouge: LSU, 1975), esp. 60–91. A comprehensive study is H.-J. Klauck, *Hausgemeinde und Hauskirche im frühen Christentum* (Stuttgarter Bibelstudien 103; Stuttgart: KBW, 1981).

[97]While most scholars agree that Philippians is authentically Pauline, many think that it is a composite letter, put together by joining smaller pieces of Pauline correspondence. Thus it is uncertain whether the Opening Formula of the letter is from Paul or from the compositor. If the latter, our sole clear Pauline evidence for the existence of bishops in the Pauline churches during Paul's lifetime would be lost.

householders to the prophets and teachers of the churches are more obscure. Did the householder teach those who came to his house? Or were prophets and teachers shared by various house churches?

We must remember that the owners of some house churches seem to have been women. "Those of Chloe" who send a report to Paul (I Cor 1:11) may be Christians who met at the house of Ms. Chloe; and Acts 12:12 suggests that Christians met at the house of Mary, the mother of John Mark.[98] I Corinthians 16:19 refers to a church meeting in the house of a couple, Aquila and Prisca. We do not know if there were women presbyters in churches in the NT period;[99] but if there were women householders and if householders had pastoral roles in the churches meeting in their houses, some of the Pauline remarks forbidding roles to women may be more intelligible. Does I Cor 14:34 specify that "women should keep silence in the churches" because men householders normally spoke and, without a specific prohibition, women householders would have had the same right? Does I Tim 2:12 specify, "I permit no woman to teach or have authority over men," because men householders were among the presbyters who had authority and taught (I Tim 5:17) and, without a specific prohibition, women householders would have had the same right? If we know that Aquila and Prisca together maintained a house where the church met, Acts 18:26 describes Priscilla and Aquila expounding the way of God more accurately to Apollos, the distinguished preacher from Alexandria.

(2) *Cultic issues.* Who baptized people in the house churches of the Pauline mission?[100] Did the householder baptize? This is not an improbable suggestion (especially as regards slaves in the household) and would help to explain the popularity of family terminology within the Christian community. We know virtually nothing about who presided at the eucharist in regional churches, although *Didache* 10:7 suggests that at the end of the century prophets were still able to hold a eucharist in the manner they wished; and by the early second century, in churches addressed

---

[98]Acts gives prominence to women patrons of Paul, e.g., at Philippi Lydia who was baptized with her whole household (16:14–15; see also 17:4,12 and 17:34 [Damaris]). It is not impossible that the Christian communities met at the home of such women.

[99]See *CMB* 141–42.

[100]This question is made more acute by Paul's statement pertinent to his year and a half at Corinth, "I baptized none of you except Crispus and Gaius. . . . Also I baptized the *house* of Stephanus" (I Cor 1:14–15).

by Ignatius, a bishop or his designate could preside. In the late NT period, when there was no prophet present, did the householder preside at the eucharist? Acts 2:46 remembers that bread was broken in the houses of Christians; and *if* the Passover model of Judaism continued to influence the eucharist, conceivably the host of the house *might have* celebrated the eucharist.

(3) *Ethical issues.* Some of the moral teaching of the NT becomes more intelligible when we concentrate on the house church as the functional Christian unit. The prominence of *Haustafeln* or Lists of Rules for the Household[101] cannot be explained simply because the family was the basic Christian unit. Most of the house directives envisage slaves and thus the very kind of house that served as the focal point for the Christian community. Careful consideration of sociology and archaeology suggests that Christians met at the houses of wealthy believers.[102] Only a fairly wealthy person would have had a "living room" large enough for the ten to forty people that constituted a house church; and the NT itself bears witness that the owners of house churches had slaves, e.g., Philemon, and Mary of Jerusalem (Acts 12:1–2).[103] The Christian eucharistic assembly in the house of a wealthy person brought into that person's living quarters people of lower status and poverty who under normal circumstances would never have been admitted. Perhaps this explains the social restiveness of Christians (I Cor 7:20–24 tells slaves to remain content as slaves), and such strange situations as that described in I Cor 11:18–21 where at the Lord's Supper only some were invited to eat a full meal (the friends of the householder and his social equals?).

I have made only superficial suggestions on a few issues pertinent to house churches; those interested in the theology of the local church will see many more possibilities (and repercussions).

---

[101]Col 3:18–4:1; Eph 5:22–6:9; I Tim 2:8–15; 6:1–2; Titus 2:1–10; I Pet 2:13–3:7.

[102]See Malherbe (footnote 96 above) 71ff.; G. Theissen, *The Social Setting of Pauline Christianity* (Philadelphia: Fortress, 1982) 69–119; J. G. Gager, *Kingdom and Community: The Social World of Early Christianity* (Englewood Cliffs, NJ: Prentice-Hall, 1975).

[103]The householders Aquila and Prisca seem to have had the money to make their way to Corinth after being expelled from Rome (Acts 18:2).

VARIOUS NEW TESTAMENT COMMUNITIES

I said above that the house churches of the Pauline mission were the simplest form of the topic since, for a while at least, the house churches in a Pauline city would have been homogeneous. However, the situation would have been quite different later in major Christian centers. In the year 90 in a place like Antioch or Ephesus, for instance, conceivably there would have been a variety of house churches resulting from different Christian missions. Let me suggest a possible range:[104]

(a) A house church of Christian Jews still insisting that acceptance of the Law was necessary for salvation, holding a low christology in which Jesus was the Messiah but not divine in origin, and celebrating the eucharist as a memorial of Jesus.

(b) A house church of mixed Jewish and Gentile Christians, stemming from a mission associated with the Jerusalem Apostles and holding the Twelve in high honor as founders of the church. While Gentiles did not need to be circumcised, the Law still had meaning for Christian life. This group would have believed in Jesus as the Son of God through virginal conception, and have stressed that the eucharist was truly the body and blood of Christ.

(c) A house church from the Pauline mission, consisting mostly of Gentiles who felt completely liberated from the Law, thinking of Paul as "the Apostle," believing in Jesus as the first-born of all creation.

(d) A Johannine house church, consisting of those who thought of themselves as God's children through birth from above and for whom birth as a Jew or Gentile was an irrelevancy of the flesh. This group would not use the title apostle but would regard all as disciples; they would not speak of the church in foundational language since Jesus was an ongoing presence to each generation through the Paraclete. Jesus would be seen as the incarnation of the divine Word spoken before creation, and the eucharist would constitute his flesh and blood which all must eat and drink if they are to share the divine life of God's unique Son.

It is not clear to what extent Christians from one of these house

---

[104]The house churches I list can be reconstructed from the NT and Ignatius of Antioch; they constitute a minimal range. For a wider range, see R. E. Brown, *The Community of the Beloved Disciple* (New York: Paulist, 1978) 168–69.

churches would be welcome at another house church. Certainly those of (a) would not be welcome at (c) or (d), and vice versa.

I am using this imagined picture to introduce another form of the local church in the NT. After the death of the great apostles in the 60s,[105] our knowledge of Christian church life is drawn from reading between the lines of Christian writings of the last third of the first century and reconstructing the communities for whom such works would make sense. These communities, even if they were made up of many house churches in many areas, may be said to constitute theologically different "local churches."

Let me offer a very brief sketch of the diverse churches or Christian communities of the postapostolic period of the NT:[106]

(1) *Three forms of post-Pauline communities.* Despite the enormous impact of Paul's personality and thought upon the churches founded in his mission, after his death those loyal to him developed distinct lines of development and interest. I shall stress below characteristic features in the ecclesiology of each of three communities; but let me caution that many other aspects of their respective theologies are distinctive. Also, I do not mean that the emphasis of one community would necessarily lead that community to deny altogether the emphasis of another community; rather it is a question of the truly operative factor in the respective conception of the church.

(a) The post-Pauline communities reflected in the Pastoral Epistles.[107] Here the traumatic questions of teaching, guidance, and survival raised by the death of the apostles are answered in terms of church structure. Getting presbyter-bishops (and deacons)[108] appointed in every

---

[105]The only three apostles about whom we have detailed knowledge from the NT are Peter (first among the Twelve), Paul (apostle of the Gentiles), and James (brother of the Lord, not a member of the Twelve)—all three died in the mid-60s, in Rome and in Jerusalem respectively.

[106]My book *Churches* (footnote 34 above) explains these church situations in detail and supplies bibliography.

[107]I use the vague term "reflected in" because sometimes we encounter a situation existing in the churches addressed and other times a situation familiar to the author (and the church where he has lived) that he wished to introduce into the churches addressed.

[108]We know nothing of what deacons did in the NT period or (since the requirements for presbyters and deacons are the same) why some people were appointed deacons and some presbyters. If the householders of NT house churches served as presbyters, could

church is the solution, for such officers will hold on to the tradition and protect against dangerous new teaching; they will constitute a regular, ongoing institution for pastoral care.

(b) The post-Pauline communities reflected in Ephesians and Colossians. Such figures as presbyter-bishops are never mentioned in these Epistles, which pay little attention to structure. Instead, there is offered an ideal of the church as the body of Christ, the spotless bride for whom he gave himself—a body that spans heaven and earth and in which the members are being constantly nourished by Christ, the head, and are growing together unto God. This is an organic, not an institutional model of the church; it offers a vision that will continue to attract people who will give themselves for the church.

(c) The post-Pauline situation reflected in Luke/Acts. (It is not clear whether Luke is writing for one church or a group of churches; it is possible that the addressees are more tangentially related to the Pauline mission than are the direct descendants addressed in the Deutero-Pauline Epistles.[109]) Here neither structure nor idealism is the operative ecclesiological factor. Church development is seen as a historical process moving from Jerusalem and the Jews to Rome and the Gentiles; at each crucial step the Holy Spirit intervenes and guides the church leaders in their decision (see p. 108 above). Presumably the death of those leaders would cause no trauma; for the Holy Spirit would continue to guide, and the church would continue to grow and spread.

(2) *Two forms of Johannine communities.* According to the author of I John 2:19, a group from the community with which he identified himself had seceded; and it is most probable that these secessionists considered themselves the true heirs of the Johannine tradition, even as did the epistolary author and his adherents. While these two communities differed among themselves as to the importance of Jesus' human career and the salvific importance of Christian life, they both probably differed from other Christians in terms of an extraordinarily high christology and of an ecclesiology that put no emphasis on structure, on apostolic foundation, and on continuity with the apostles. The Johannine ideal seems

---

there have been a socio-economic distinction: those who did not own houses large enough for community meetings became deacons?

[109]Luke/Acts does not identify its author, and today many careful scholars doubt the accuracy of the late 2nd-century guess that the author was Luke, a companion of Paul.

to have been a community of equal disciples receiving God's life from Christ—children of God living in *koinōnia* with the Son and the Father, who need no human teacher, for they are taught by the Paraclete. (I shall not go into detail here, but there are significant Johannine differences from any of the three post-Pauline concepts listed above.)

(3) *A community related to I Peter.* A community where Peter is venerated and where the basic preaching is shaped by Jewish symbolism, especially that of the Exodus. The church is seen as a renewed Israel fulfilling God's promises to Israel in the desert: a chosen race, a royal priesthood, a holy nation, God's own people (I Pet 2:9). The officers of the community are the presbyters (elders) and the younger (= deacons; 5:5).

(4) *The Matthean community.* A mixed community of Jews and Gentiles, observing the Law as interpreted by Jesus, honoring Peter as the rock on which the church has been built, possessing authoritative teachers and lines of authority, but anxious to make authority conform to the spirit of Jesus who protected the little ones and was willing to forgive seventy times seven.

(5) *A community related to the Epistle of James.* A very Jewish community in outlook for whom the name of James the brother of the Lord had authority. A practical insistence on works of piety (caring for the widows and orphans) marks this group which seems to assemble in a Christianized synagogue.

(6) *Other communities.* A longer discussion would need to consider Mark, Hebrews, and Revelation in order to determine how one might speak about the communities addressed by these works or represented by the author of these works. And since *Didache, I Clement,* and perhaps even Ignatius of Antioch would be contemporary with some NT works, one might wish to introduce the ecclesiology of these subapostolic writers into a discussion of theological communities as "local churches" of the NT period.

THE CHURCHES OF GREAT CHRISTIAN CENTERS

Another aspect of the study of local churches would be the history of Christianity in a single city over a period of time, from the NT period into the 2nd century. Among attempts in this direction have been a study of Rome and Ephesus[110] as representing two different styles of Christian ecclesiology and christology, and a study of Rome and Jerusalem[111] as representing two different ideals. Recently specific aspects of the church of Antioch have been studied.[112] Let me take the example of the church of Rome and show how modern biblical studies might contribute to the study of this local church, complementing what has been known from history and archaeology.[113]

Christ had been preached in Rome (almost surely by disciples from Jerusalem) by the mid-40s, and there was a thriving Roman Christian community when Paul wrote Romans about 58. *I Clement* was written from the church of Rome to the church of Corinth about forty years later, presumably by a presbyter of Rome. In the forty-year interval between Romans and *I Clement,* I Peter was probably written from Rome (5:13: "She who is at Babylon") to Gentile Christians of northern Asia Minor, and Hebrews was probably written to Rome (13:24: "Those from Italy greet you"). From these four works what might one reconstruct of the Roman church?

A Jewish emphasis seems to remain strong throughout the period even as the Gentiles increase in number. In Romans, Paul takes extraordinary care to make clear that his gospel is not different from the early Jewish formulation of the gospel known to Rome,[114] that he has never denied the special privileges of the Jews (9:4–5), and that the preaching to the Gentiles did not displace the Jews in God's plan of salvation. (What an extraordinary statement for Paul: that he converted Gentiles to make the Jews envious, and that the Gentiles were only a wild olive branch grafted on the tree of Israel [11:13–14, 24]!) Romans may contain

---

[110]K. Lake, *Landmarks in the History of Early Christianity* (New York: Macmillan, 1922) 75–103.

[111]H. von Campenhausen and H. Chadwick, *Jerusalem and Rome* (Facet Books Historical Series #4; Philadelphia: Fortress, 1966).

[112]W. A. Meeks and R. L. Wilken, *Jews and Christians in Antioch* (SBL Sources for Biblical Study 13; Missoula: Scholars Press, 1978). J. P. Meier traces the development of Antiochene Christianity in *AR*.

[113]In *AR* I have traced in detail the development of the church of Rome in the first century.

[114]It is generally agreed that Rom 1:3–4 is pre-Pauline and that the phrase "spirit of holiness" reflects Hebrew grammar; see *MNT* 34–40.

a *captatio benevolentiae* designed to make Paul acceptable among a community dominated by a Jewish Christian heritage, possibly suspicious of him. It is interesting that in Romans 3:24–25 Paul phrases redemption in the language of Jewish cultic sacrifice: "God presented Jesus as an atoning sacrifice [*hilastērion*] through faith in his blood."

In I Pet 1:13–2:10 the Roman theology of conversion and baptismal entrance into the renewed Israel is presented as an encouragement to the Gentiles addressed in Asia Minor. The analogy of the departure from Egypt and the experience of becoming a covenanted people at Sinai dominate the picture, and once more there appears the language of Jewish sacrifice: "You know that you were ransomed . . . with the precious blood of Christ, like that of a lamb without blemish or spot" (1:18–19).

The Epistle to the Hebrews may have been written to Rome shortly after the destruction of Jerusalem in 70 in order to persuade those of Jewish heritage that they should not now expect the eschatological restoration of Jewish cult in a purified Christian form. Paul's Epistle to the Romans may have persuaded them that ultimately the Jews would be converted, and they may have imagined that this would mean a purified cult, priesthood, and sacrifice. Hebrews proclaims that the cult, sacrifices, and priesthood of Israel are finished, and that the only Holy Place is in heaven, where Christ "has entered once for all, taking . . . his own blood, thus securing an eternal redemption" (9:12).

The Christian community at Rome apparently received Hebrews, for *I Clement* betrays knowledge of it. However, its message was domesticated and interpreted in a way that would have surprised its author. *I Clement* represents not the abolition of Israelite cult by Christ (the message of Hebrews), but the reintroduction of the symbolism of Israelite cult and an application to Christian realities. "God commanded us to celebrate sacrifices and services . . . at fixed times and hours. . . . For to the high priest his proper ministrations are allotted, and to the priests the proper place has been appointed, and on levites their proper services have been imposed" (50:2, 5). A few verses later *I Clement* describes how Christ appointed apostles who in turn appointed bishops and deacons (42:1–4); and while *I Clement* does not connect these ideas, it is rightly considered the forerunner of identifying the Christian bishop, presbyter, and deacons as high priest, priests, and levites, when later a triform ministry developed. Ultimately the Jewish Christian aspiration will triumph in its own way; for the eucharist will be considered the

Christian sacrifice fulfilling Mal 1:11, the episcopate and then the presbyterate will be the Christian cultic priesthood, and the Christian place of worship will be the Christian temple containing the living presence of the Son of God.[115] The conservatism of Roman Christianity, inherited from its Jewish origins, can be traced into the second century in the opposition of the Roman church to innovative theologians from the East (Valentinus, Marcion, Tatian) and in the reluctance to accept the Gospel of John (the Alogoi, Gaius?) with its adventuresome christology.

TYPES OF JEWISH/GENTILE CHRISTIANITY

Let me provide one more NT contribution to the discussion of local church by moving back to the beginnings of the spread of Christianity and commenting on the diversities in the missionary movements that brought local churches into being. As I investigated the origins of the church at Rome, I kept encountering the suggestion that after A.D. 49,[116] in place of the dominant Jewish Christianity that had hitherto existed at Rome, there was now a dominant Gentile Christianity. Whether defensible or not, such a claim is intelligible if the ethnic origin of the respective Christians is the issue. Very often, however, the affirmation stresses a friction between the two types of Christianity[117] with the likely implication that two different Christian ways of thought were involved. Indeed, once I became alert to this issue, further reading convinced me that perhaps a majority of writers are using "Jewish Christian" and

---

[115]The author of Hebrews probably never thought of such developments; and so in the technical sense they are not contradictions of his thought, even though it is quite dubious that he would have approved of them. In my judgment, Hebrews cannot be used today to demand an undoing of church developments about priesthood (in the manner of Küng), but it remains a conscience about the primacy of Christ's priesthood and the danger of obscuring that primacy when too much honor is paid to human cultic priests.

[116]This is the approximate date of Claudius' expulsion of Jews from Rome "because of their constant disturbances impelled by Chrestus [Christ?]" (Suetonius, *Claudius,* 25.4).

[117]For example, O. Cullmann, *Peter: Disciple, Apostle, Martyr* (2d ed; London: SCM, 1962) 105: ". . . frictions between the Jewish Christian and Gentile Christian sections of the Roman church." J. C. Beker, *Paul the Apostle* (Philadelphia: Fortress, 1980) 61: "It is possible that Romans 14 and 15 reflect a church in which returning Jewish Christians found a preponderance of Gentile Christians, a situation that led to friction among them."

"Gentile Christian" to differentiate theological and/or ecclesiological stances *in NT times*. (Most frequently "Gentle Christian" seems to represent a stance close to Paul's, and "Jewish Christian" a stance opposed to his.) Such a distinction may be justifiable in the second century when "the church catholic"[118] was increasingly composed of ethnic Gentiles with little history of direct contact with a Jewish heritage and when Jewish Christians were a minority distinguished by a stubborn adherence to Jewish practices (an adherence now with some frequency being dubbed heretical). But I would argue that during most of the first century a theological distinction signaled by "Jewish Christianity" and "Gentile Christianity" is imprecise and poorly designated. Rather *one can discern from the NT at least four different types of Jewish/Gentile Christianity,* stemming from the fact that Jewish Christians of different persuasions converted Gentiles who shared the respective theology of their missionaries. Let me briefly substantiate that claim.

Even those who are skeptical about the historicity of Acts tend to allow that the opening scene of Acts 6 contains a historical nucleus.[119] At Jerusalem the Hellenists are *Jewish*[120] believers in Christ who differ from the Hebrews (other *Jewish* believers in Christ who by implication in 8:1 include the apostles) in three surmisable factors:[121] (a) Hellenist Christians speak (only?) Greek, while Hebrew Christians speak Hebrew and/or Aramaic (and presumably sometimes Greek as well); (b) Hellenists come from families more acculturated to a Greco-Roman world who name their sons Stephen, Prochorus, Nicanor, as distinct from Hebrew families who name them Johanan (John), Simeon (Simon), Judah (Judas), etc.; (c) Hellenist Christians do not believe that God dwells in the Jerusalem Temple (exclusively?—see 7:47–51), while Hebrew Christians continue frequently to go to the Temple for worship (2:46; 3:1;

---

[118]Ignatius, *Smyrn.* 8:2.

[119]The admission that there was strife runs against Luke's stress on Christian one-mindedness (ten times in Acts), and 6:2 offers the only instance in Acts where Luke speaks of the apostles as "the Twelve."

[120]The fact that Nicolaus is identified as a proselyte suggests that the other six Hellenist leaders in Acts 6:5 were natural-born Jews.

[121]The factors that distinguish Hellenists from Hebrews are disputed; so also is whether Paul was deemed a Hebrew (by Luke) and whether most NT Christians would have known this distinction with which Luke was familiar. See the discussions in *AR* 6–7, 34, 140 for the rationale.

5:42). In the subsequent story of Acts, Hellenist Jewish Christians convert non-Jews to Christianity, e.g., Samaritans (8:4–6) and Gentiles (11:19–20).[122] Surely the non-Jewish Christians thus converted shared the attitude toward Jewish cult that characterized their missionaries.

Hebrew Christians, however, also converted Gentiles and so produced a Jewish/Gentile Christianity different from the Jewish/Gentile Christianity produced by the Hellenist missionaries. Or, to be exact, one should say that Hebrew Christians produced several non-Hellenist types of Jewish/Gentile Christianity, for Hebrew Christians were not all of one mind. Let me begin describing the diversity within Hebrew Christianity by making a case that Paul was a Hebrew Christian, not a Hellenist Christian. In the only other NT instances of the term "Hebrew" besides Acts 6:1, Paul twice calls himself a Hebrew (II Cor 11:22; Phil 3:5). If one argues that for Paul the term may mean simply "Jew" and not necessarily have the Acts' connotation of Hebrew vs. Hellenist, one should note that both Pauline passages emphasize the purity of his Jewish status (a present status in II Cor 11:22: "So am I"). According to the criteria of Acts (surmised above) Paul is not a Hellenist: (a) he speaks Hebrew (22:2); (b) he bears a Jewish name, Saul; (c) he goes to the Jerusalem Temple (21:26; 24:11). Indeed, the author of Acts (who knew something about the Hellenists) tells us that Paul disputed with the Hellenists (9:29). If, then, Paul was a Hebrew, not a Hellenist, the fact that he and his Jewish companions (Timothy, Prisca, and Aquila; see also Rom 16:7) made many Gentile converts inevitably produced a Jewish/Gentile Christianity different from that of the Hellenists.

Yet there were other Hebrew Christians in Jerusalem who differed from Paul in theological outlook, and they too made Gentile converts. Both Galatians 2 and Acts 15 describe a Hebrew Christian group at Jerusalem (those of the circumcision; Christian Pharisees; false brethren) who vociferously attacked Paul because he did not demand circumcision and they believed that Gentile converts to Christianity had to be circumcised. The contention that such people were not interested in a mission to the Gentiles contradicts the implications of Acts 15:1, 24 that they had been trying to impose on Gentiles *outside Jerusalem* their demands for full observance of the Mosaic Law, including circumcision. Galatians

---

[122]The contrast with "Jews" in 11:19 virtually demands the reading "Gentiles" (Greeks) in 11:20 rather then "Hellenists."

and chap. 3 of Philippians constitute proof that Jewish Christians of this mentality conducted a mission at least in Asia Minor and in Greece and had considerable success with Gentiles (if we can judge from Paul's alarm).[123]

The recognition of a Pauline type of Jewish/Gentile Christianity and a circumcision-insistent type of Jewish/Gentile Christianity does not exhaust the variety of Hebrew Christianity discernible in the NT. Acts 15 and Galatians 2 agree that Peter and James were open to converting Gentiles without demanding circumcision. Yet James or "men from James" insisted that Gentile converts in dealings with Jewish Christians respect certain Jewish purity laws, especially with regard to food (Acts 15:20; Gal 2:12). In both accounts, although such observances were not Peter's idea, he acquiesced and they were enforced at Antioch,[124] even though Paul violently disagreed—in fact, he never *imposed* them at Corinth (I Cor 8:1–13). The logic of these events is that there emerged a Jewish/Gentile Christianity associated with James and Peter[125] (and with Jerusalem origins) which was intermediate between that of Paul and that of his missionary opponents in Galatia and Philippi.

The observation made above about differences between (several varieties of) Hebrew Christians and Hellenist (Jewish) Christians and about

---

[123]My colleague at Union Theological Seminary, J. L. Martyn, has given several public lectures (anticipating his commentary on Galatians in the Anchor Bible) explaining convincingly that there was an active law-observant mission to the Gentiles, not just scattered opposition to Paul, and why it would have been attractive.

[124]In support of Gal 2:11–13, note that Acts 15:23 incorporates "the apostles" (which has to include Peter) in the letter enforcing James' ideas on Antioch (Syria and Cilicia). In my judgment, Acts 15 is a composite scene; and the purity-laws part of the Jerusalem decision was *in later reaction* to what transpired in Antioch, as described in Gal 2:11ff. In any case Paul's position did not win the day at Antioch. See Meier, *AR* 39.

[125]Peter was more central than James in the active thrust of this mission to the Gentiles. True, Gal 2:7 assigns to Peter the mission "to the circumcised"; but that is directly contrary to Acts 15:7, and the latter is probably truer to the *total career* of Peter who in his later years may have been very active in Gentile circles. The possibility that he went to Corinth is raised by I Cor 9:5, and the "Cephas party" at Corinth (1:12) scarcely consisted only of Jewish Christians. The direction of I Peter to Gentile Christians in northern Asia Minor makes little sense unless, in the tradition, Peter converted Gentiles. (Note that the Epistle of James is directed to Jewish Christians.)

the missions to the Gentiles directed by the respective forms of Jewish Christianity can be schematized into the following discernible types of Jewish/Gentile Christianity:[126]

TYPE ONE: Jewish Christians and their Gentile converts who practiced full observance of the Mosaic Law, including circumcision, as necessary for receiving the fullness of the salvation brought by Jesus Christ. This movement, which originated in Jerusalem, had some success in Galatia and Philippi, and perhaps elsewhere.

TYPE TWO: Jewish Christians and their Gentile converts who did not insist on circumcision as salvific for Gentile Christians but did require them to keep some Jewish purity laws. This movement, which also originated in Jerusalem, was associated with James and Peter. It became the dominant Christianity of Antioch and probably of Rome, Pontus, Cappadocia, and sections of the Province of Asia.[127]

TYPE THREE: Jewish Christians and their Gentile converts who did not insist on circumcision as salvific for Gentile Christians and did not require their observing Jewish purity laws in regard to food. (It is likely that both Type Two and Type Three insisted on Jewish purity laws forbidding marriage among kin since I Cor 5:1 and Acts 15:20, 29 are probably rejecting the same form of *porneia*.) Antioch was originally the departure point of this mission, and Paul and the companions mentioned in his letters[128] were its most famous spokesmen in the West. According to Acts 20:16; 21:26; 24:11, this type of Christianity did not entail a break with the cultic practices of Judaism (feasts, Temple), nor did it impel *Jewish* Christians to abandon circumcision and the Law.[129]

---

[126]This minimal listing is discussed in more detail in *AR* 1–9. See traces of still further Christian diversity in footnote 95 above.

[127]These localities are deduced from I Peter, but is it accidental that they are also in the list of Acts 2:9–10? That list may reflect places evangelized by the Jerusalem Christianity associated with the Jerusalem apostles and the brothers of the Lord.

[128]After A.D. 49 Paul's earlier companions, Barnabas and John Mark, seem to have aligned themselves with a mission closer to the Christianity of Type Two (Gal 2:13; Acts 15:39).

[129]See Acts 16:3 (circumcision of Timothy) and the false charge against Paul in 21:21 to be corrected by 21:24. Although many scholars think Acts inaccurate on this, Rom 2:25–3:2 and 4:2 see value (not necessity) in circumcision for the Jew if accompanied by faith, and 9:4 lists Israelite worship positively. True, the Paul of Galatians is more radical, veer-

TYPE FOUR: Jewish Christians and their Gentile converts who did not insist on circumcision and Jewish food laws and saw no abiding significance in the cult of the Jerusalem Temple. (Only this type is properly Hellenist in contrast to the three preceding varieties of "Hebrew Christianity"; indeed, only this type may be considered fully non-law-observant.) The movement began at Jerusalem, spread to Samaria with Philip, and eventually to Phoenicia, Cyprus, and Antioch (11:19–20). A later, more widespread, more radicalized variety of this type of Christianity is encountered in the Fourth Gospel and the Epistle to the Hebrews[130] where levitical sacrifices and priesthood are considered abrogated and the feasts have become alien "feasts of the Jews," so that Judaism has become another religion belonging to the old covenant.[131]

If I may return to the issue that opened this section, in light of this classification the reader can see why I regard it as theologically meaningless to be told that at Rome Jewish Christianity was replaced or outnumbered by Gentile Christianity, so that there was friction. More meaningful is this issue: Which type of Jewish Christianity first came to Rome? Earlier in the chapter I have indicated the answer I would give, but one would need to ask the same question about all the large Christian centers of the first century. The diverse missionary origins of these "local churches" may account for later differences among them. That observation may be worth keeping in mind as we discuss the emerging doctrine of the local church in Roman Catholicism today.

---

ing toward what I have designated Type Four of Jewish/Gentile Christianity, but in Romans Paul is not too far from aspects of Type Two. I plead guilty to scholarly *lèse-majesté* in finding inconsistencies between Galatians and Romans and in daring to think that Paul could change his mind.

[130]The Hellenist sermon of Stephen in Acts 7:44 treats the desert Tabernacle positively; for both John (1:14: *skēnoun*) and Hebrews, Jesus replaces the Tabernacle.

[131]For Paul, Christians of Type One are "false brothers" (Gal 2:4). John despises the crypto-Christians in the synagogue who do not confess Jesus publicly (12:42—a later species of Type One?) as well as the brothers of the Lord (7:5—more conservative Christians of Type Two, associated posthumously with James?).

Chapter 8
THE PREACHING DESCRIBED IN THE BOOK OF ACTS AS A GUIDE TO EARLY CHRISTIAN DOCTRINAL PRIORITIES

I have stressed in this book that there is a trajectory from the NT studied critically to the developed doctrines of later Christianity. I do not mean by that, however, that there was incomplete Christian doctrine in the first century in regard to teachings and emphases crucial for faith and life. The developed articulation of doctrine at a later period was in response to questions that had been raised in the subsequent centuries, but this development did not necessarily produce a greater faith or a holier life. From the start the proclamation of the gospel opened people to salvific faith and deep holiness of life. It occurred to me that it might be useful to give an example of what may be said to pass as "doctrine" or better, doctrinal priorities in the first Christian century. Rather than attempting a global NT description, let me concentrate on the sermons in the Acts of the Apostles.[132]

In fidelity to biblical criticism, when I am describing preaching in Acts, I am very conscious that in the sermons we do not necessarily have the words of Peter or Paul or Stephen. We have unquestionably the words of the unknown author of the Book of Acts[133] who dramatizes for his readers Peter and Paul and Stephen speaking on certain occasions. (We can only guess about his sources and their accuracy; yet the primary

---

[132]In particular, the sermons of Peter in Acts 2; 3; 5; 10; the sermons of Paul in Acts 13; 17; and the sermon of Stephen in Acts 7.

[133]See footnote 109 above.

interest of an interpreter is not sources but what the author of the Book
of Acts has written.) I insist on this because otherwise one might get the
facile impression that we are actually reading the first sermons ever
given by Christians. We are not. We are reading sermons composed by
an author, perhaps in the 80s of the first century, to convey a message
to his audience. Note: "to *his* audience." We are not hearing sermons
addressed to us, but sermons once addressed to an audience in the 80s.
The idea that the Scriptures are written *to* us is a mistake that leads to
the distortion of the word of God. The Scriptures have meaning *for* us,
but they were written to audiences that lived at the time of their authors.

Having stressed the historical conditioning of the preaching in the
Book of Acts, allow me to draw another observation. Hebrew *dabar* that
we translate as "word" has a much wider meaning, including "thing"
and "action." If one would study the Book of Acts, one must realize
that preaching is only a partial element of what an author with a biblical
background would think of by the "word" of God. Acts describes the
actions of the apostolic preachers, including their healings of the sick,
their raisings of the dead, their sufferings, and even their martyrdoms.
Such an emphasis on actions is important to remember. Frankly, I rejoice
in the fact that Roman Catholic clergy are not called preachers. The failure to designate them thus may indicate all too sadly that Catholics do
not put enough emphasis on preaching, but there is a greater distortion
involved in identifying clergy as if their only task were to preach. The
early Christian proclaimers of the Good News did more than preach, and
we had better do more in this world than preach if we wish to be proclaimers of the word of God. As has often been said, the God of Israel
is a God who acts and not simply a God who speaks. Both descriptions
are anthropomorphic, but nevertheless together they convey the truth
that those who proclaim the God of Israel and the Father of Jesus Christ
had better be as concerned about action as about preaching.

DIVERSITIES IN THE SERMONS

After such preliminary cautions I now move toward my main concern: the sermons in the Acts of the Apostles. Since they are all com-
positions of the author of Acts, not surprisingly there are common
features. The surprise is rather the amount of diversity we find among
the sermons. Perhaps such diversity is explicable because the author had

sources reflecting diverse traditions, but just as plausible is the thesis that the author had great skill in adjusting his sermon composition to different situations. In either case, the diversity of the sermons in Acts teaches us something about doctrinal expression. There are some wrong ways, but no totally exclusive right way to preach the word of God. Rather, with all its splendor, the word of God requires a diversity of presentation, reflecting different ways in which God's revelation can have meaning in human life.

First, there is diversity on the part of the preacher. The author of Acts describes Peter on several occasions going to the Temple in Jerusalem and preaching Jesus Christ there (3:1; 5:12). The author makes it clear that the setting is part of the piety of the apostles who were among those whom he describes as "every day in the Temple" (5:42). Nevertheless, the author also gives us a sermon by Stephen who does not believe that God dwells in the Temple. Rather, in building the Temple the Israelites were offending against the will of God who does not dwell in human houses; and thus they were resisting the Holy Spirit (7:48–51). In other words Acts describes as proclaiming the word of God with equal piety preachers whose views on the relation of the Christian message to the Jerusalem Temple were virtually contradictory. (The attitude of the author of Acts may not be far from that of Paul in Phil 2:15–18: "Some indeed preach Christ from envy and rivalry, but others from good will. . . . What then? Only that in every way . . . Christ is proclaimed.") Whether or not the preachers of Acts had the same view of the Jerusalem Temple, they shared a view of the centrality of Christ; and for Acts that centrality was all important in evaluating their proclamation of the word. I point to this diversity and centrality as of possible value for our preaching and teaching today. Not every view can be proclaimed from our pulpits; but particularly in Roman Catholicism the desire for absolute uniformity in the conception of the Christian message may not be true to the NT itself which allowed a diversity among Christians who still shared *koinōnia,* or "communion," with one another. We must realize that on many theological issues Peter and Paul and Stephen could disagree violently, and yet they were all esteemed by the author of Acts as great Christian witnesses and preachers. A range of diversity is both allowed and demanded by the word of God.

A second aspect of the diversity in Acts, this time affecting the audience, is reflected in Paul's preaching in chap. 13 to the "men of Israel," where he introduces his words about Christ by reciting the history of Israel.[134] In Acts 17 the same Paul addresses the "men of Athens," speaking to them about the Lord of heaven and earth who gives life to all and governs the course of all nations. In other words, for the author of Acts there are two different Pauline prefaces to the Christian proclamation, one for Jews, the other for Gentiles. I have insisted from the beginning of this book that the word of God depends not only on God but also on the human beings for whom this has to be a word. Woe to those responsible for formulating the word of God as doctrine if what is contained therein is not "of God," but also woe to them if it is not truly a word because it has not been made meaningful to the audience to whom they address the divine message.

Granted that the "men of Athens" can be addressed without a recitation of what we may call the OT story, it is still remarkable how often the author of Acts makes the OT story a part of the preaching almost equal in length to the story of Jesus Christ. In Acts 2 Peter does not specifically turn his message to Jesus of Nazareth until he has recalled the words of Joel the prophet; and even when he does turn to Jesus, the words of the psalmist are part of the message about Jesus. In Acts 7 Stephen traces the story of Israel from Abraham to Solomon in a long sermon that never even gets to Jesus Christ other than by implication. In Acts 13 Paul spends more than half his sermon on what the God of Israel has done before he announces that this God has brought to Israel "a Savior, Jesus." These are sermons that Acts addresses to the Jews or to "men of Israel," but perhaps one can draw from them implications for a message addressed to the people of God today, a people for whom the OT is by church teaching as much the Scriptures of God as the NT. Too often for Christians the proclamation of the word means the proclamation of the Jesus story. Yet that story can be easily misconstrued and distorted if one does not also recite the story of Israel. For instance, the triumph of what has been accomplished in Jesus Christ and the success it should have in the world is a dangerous message if one has not heard the story of God's salvific acts in Israel, including the decimation of His people and the loss of the land and of the Temple. The word of God can be as truly proclaimed in defeat as in victory when that defeat warns us of the

---

[134]Here the translation "men" is warranted, not careless, because the Greek is *andres*, not *anthrōpoi*.

possibility of confusing our success with what God regards as success. Such a message does not always become clear in the NT, written in a short period of spreading and seemingly victorious faith; it comes through very clearly in the OT story, a millennium long, which allows us to see the interplay between God's message and human appropriation and distortion.

THE MESSAGE ABOUT CHRIST

While insisting on the importance of the OT preface, one would have to say that a comparison of the main sermons in Acts leads firmly to the centrality of Jesus Christ in the proclamation of the word. What God has done in Christ from the time of his baptism through mighty deeds, leading to the crucifixion of Christ by men and his resurrection by God—this is certainly for the author of Acts the heart of the message. The very fact that the author mentions that those who accepted this proclamation were soon called Christians means that it is inconceivable that Christ is not the primary proclamation. If I may be permitted to draw from this a lesson for our priorities today, I would insist that what God did in Jesus Christ must still be the heart of our message. That does not mean that we can ignore implications about what *we are to do* toward God and toward humanity; but all such obligation of action depends on understanding and believing in Jesus Christ. It would be fascinating to take a poll of the people in our churches and ask them what it means today to be a Christian. Many "Bible Christians" might answer, "Have faith in Jesus as Savior," and fail to include the obligation of loving others. A greater number of Christians, not doctrinally concerned, might answer in existential terms about what one must do, for instance, in terms of loving one's neighbor. Existential demand is urgent—Christians must love—but our *behavior is not a sufficiently differentiating element in the definition of a Christian.* Christians are those who have a clear faith about Jesus of Nazareth, that he is the Christ, the Messiah of God. Any definition of a Christian that does not involve a clear proclamation of who Jesus is (alongside the obligation of loving) fails the criterion of the first proclamations of Christianity. Indeed, in this aspect, Christianity has a certain uniqueness among the religions of the world. For all their reverence for Moses, Jews would not define their religion in terms of who Moses is. Muslims resent the appellation "Mohammedans'' because they regard this as a distortion of their religion along the lines of Christian thought patterns: their primary faith is about Allah for whom Mohammed was a prophet. But we Christians are people whose definition comes, not simply in terms of what we say about God, but in terms of what we say about Jesus, precisely because we think that we cannot understand God unless we understand who Jesus was and is. The failure to proclaim Jesus and what God did in him will eviscerate the Christian proclamation of the word of God.

In the sermons of Acts, it is clear that the crucifixion and resurrection represent the heart of the story of Jesus. Particularly from Acts 2 and Acts 10 we can learn a lesson about what it means to make Jesus Christ the center of the proclamation. One cannot proclaim him without the resurrection, which was God's vindication of Jesus. The oldest formulations of the Christian creedal faith may be imbedded in these sermons in the Book of Acts, particularly in the antithesis: You killed him, but God raised him up. These proclaim a divine action and a divine victory. Such a proclamation shows that Christianity is not primarily a religion of human possibilities or of what we can do; it is primarily a proclamation of God's action and of His grace reversing our sinfulness and weakness.

If the resurrection is the divine action most clearly expressing this victory, that resurrection in the sermons of Acts makes little sense without the cross. At times, when I wish to portray this point bluntly, I tell people that Jesus could have been victorious over death if he died of a heart attack on the shores of the Lake of Galilee and if subsequently God raised him up; but then Christianity would be a different religion. The author of Acts caught the essential contrast, the essential paradox of Christianity, namely, victory *after the disgraceful kind of death Jesus died*. Dying after being betrayed by his disciple and rejected by the religious leaders was part of Jesus' revelation of God's kingdom. It is no accident that, when we have sought visually to portray Christianity, the cross has been our clearest sign. Without the resurrection the cross would be meaningless; but without the cross the resurrection might confirm a triumphalistic human understanding of God rather than God's self-understanding.

Even if the cross and the resurrection are the central aspect of the christology of the sermons in Acts, the ministry of Jesus is also important. In the NT, Paul is the author who most uses the word ''gospel'';

yet Paul rarely quotes the words or deeds of the ministry of Jesus. His concentration is on the death and resurrection of Jesus: "Put to death for our trespasses and raised for our justification" (Rom 4:25). Nevertheless, it seems that the church has not accepted the narrow confines of the Pauline understanding of gospel; for she has placed in the canon of the NT before the Pauline letters four other works entitled "Gospels." They concentrate on the ministry of Jesus and indeed give greater proportion to that ministry than to the story of the cross and resurrection. For most people, a reference to a Gospel is a reference to one of these four works. Perhaps this attitude is adumbrated in Acts in the sermons that tell first of what God did in Jesus from the time of the baptism before they turn to the crucifixion and resurrection. For instance, the sermon in Acts 2 speaks of "mighty wonders and works and signs which God did through him in your midst." The sermon in Acts 10 speaks of his "being anointed with the Holy Spirit and with power" and his "doing good, and healing all that were afflicted." Indeed, if as I have said already, one cannot understand the resurrection properly without the cross, one cannot understand either the cross or the resurrection without understanding the Jesus who reached out to heal the sick and to give mobility to the lame. Moreover, if one wishes to go beyond the sermons of Acts, I would argue that one cannot understand the cross and resurrection properly without realizing that it is the death and victory of one who proclaimed God's blessing to the poor and the oppressed. In all this, we are taught the centrality of the *whole picture* of Jesus Christ, his life, death, and resurrection.

REACTION TO THE MESSAGE

If this is the fundamental Christian proclamation, if this is the gospel, if this is the word of God understood both as deed and preached word (the Hebrew *dabar* that I mentioned above), the sermon in Acts 2 does not leave us without a description of the necessary reaction to the proclamation or gospel or word of God. In 2:37 those who hear the message of Peter say to him and to the rest of the apostles, "Brothers, what shall we do?" The first demand that Peter places by way of response is *Metanoēsate*. Most translations render this as "Repent"; a few go further and translate it as "Change your lives." The literal Greek meaning of *metanoein,* however, is "to change one's mind." Unless we understand the fullness of that term, we cannot understand why or how the word of God constitutes an offense. It is true that, if one is a serious sinner, ''to change one's mind'' or ''to change one's way of thinking'' means ''to repent'' or ''to change one's way of living.'' But most Christian proclamation of the word of God today is addressed to those who are not conscious of being serious sinners. Is either the preacher or the audience to think that the obligations of *metanoein* have been accomplished simply because serious sin is not an issue? Such misapprehension will not occur if we understand *metanoein* to mean ''to change one's mind.''

Religious people think they know what God wants. If one suggests to such people that it is necessary to change one's mind about what God wants in order to hear the word of God, then the offense of the Gospel becomes clear. We remember that Jesus had few problems with sinners; they seem to have been relatively open to his message. His greatest problem was with religious people who knew already what God wanted and were therefore offended by hearing a different message from Jesus. The Christian preachers in the Book of Acts are portrayed as placing the same demand that Jesus placed. True, they placed this demand upon people who were hearing the gospel for the first time; but one may well ask if *Metanoēsate* is not an enduring demand for hearing the gospel at any time. The preacher who asks people to change their minds is often the preacher who will be castigated for disturbing the people, precisely because it is not sufficiently stressed that Jesus was a disturbing figure and that his message presented faithfully will inevitably disturb. That disturbance does not touch simply sinful behavior but also wrong conceptions of God's set of values and wrong understanding of doctrines.

I see this as a particular problem in the experience of Roman Catholics. We have been emphatic that we have a set of answers and that those need to be repeated and passed on from generation to generation. The whole catechism approach implies that. I do not deny that we have a continuous truth, but that truth needs to be rephrased in every generation if it is to be effective. The idea of rephrasing revealed truth is *not* the innovation of radical theologians; it is acknowledged by Rome itself (see p. 29 above). Walking the narrow line between carelessly or needlessly disturbing people and the necessary challenge and disturbance caused by the gospel properly preached is a very difficult task—a task not helped by ultraconservatives who charge every new presentation or new idea with being dangerous. The gospel insistence on changing one's mind repeated after the sermon in Acts 2 is an enduring statement that the greatest danger facing religion is *not* the danger of new ideas; it is *the danger of no ideas at all.* Too often those who have the official task of proclaiming the word of God see no danger if people are passively content in their religion. They see a greater danger when people are restive about what they hear and when they ask themselves and others challenging questions. Such a fearful attitude is not faithful to the fundamental reaction demanded by the preaching of Jesus and his followers in terms of *metanoein.*

After insisting on repentance or change of mind, in Acts 2:38 Peter places a demand that Jesus is never remembered as placing during his public ministry, namely, the demand to be baptized. Jesus was not a baptizer; yet those who proclaimed his gospel insisted on the necessity of being baptized (see p. 46 above). One sees here a new aspect of the proclamation of the gospel. Even though there was a collective force to the gospel preached by Jesus in his lifetime, he simply presupposed Israel and the whole people of God as the context of his message. Hence, although he associated with himself a group of disciples, Jesus was not clearly shaping *an organized society* by his preaching; there was no "church" in his public ministry;[135] there was Israel which he was calling to change its mind. Yet Acts portrays the Christian preachers as immediately beginning to form a society within Israel. The insistence on baptism is a very important mark of the structuring of a society—one now has a way of knowing openly those who accepted the proclamation. The believers are baptized visibly and thus enter a *koinōnia,* "communion" with one another. This may be one aspect of the word of God that is sometimes neglected in the modern conception of the desirable effects of preaching. The proclamation of Christianity has as its goal not simply personal conversion or personal change of mind; it has as its goal the formation and development of the church, the people of God. It is true that in the Gospel of John baptism is portrayed in terms of being begotten from above or born again of water and Spirit;[136] but that is not the por-

---

[135]I have pointed out above (p. 60) that this historical fact does not vitiate the doctrine that Christ founded the church; it simply demands nuance in understanding that doctrine.

[136]Even the Fourth Gospel is not purely individualistic, however; for the concepts of the flock of sheep in John 10 and of the vine in John 15 (both of them images used for Israel) presuppose that Christians belong to a collectivity, whether or not that collectivity was called church in Johannine language (see p. 117 above).

trayal in Acts. For the author of Acts baptism involves acceptance into a community, and Christianity is a communitarian religion. To all those people who say, "Jesus is my personal savior," I would insist (without negating the personal element in the salvation wrought by Jesus) that our primary understanding must be that of Jesus *saving a people*. This emphasis makes proclaiming the word of God or communicating doctrine a church-related task, so that the effectiveness of preaching must be evaluated in terms not simply of how many hearts are touched, but also of how the church is built up.

The demand to be baptized in Acts 2:38 is continued with a further comment about purpose: "Be baptized every one of you in the name of Jesus Christ for the forgiveness of your sins." I spoke as strongly as I could above of the centrality of belief in Jesus Christ as part of the definition of a Christian. If baptism has its communal effect, that effect is related to the fact that the person to be baptized makes a confession of who Jesus is, of his name: He is the Christ (Messiah), the Lord, the Savior, the Son of God (Acts 2:36; 5:31; 13:33). And this baptism and confession of Jesus Christ is accompanied by the forgiveness of sins. The collective aspect of baptism does not obscure its personal effect; and that effect is forgiveness of sins and thus the possibility of holiness. A proclamation of the word of God that involves change of mind and baptism would still not be complete unless it also effected at least incipiently the ultimate demand of the God of Israel: "You must be holy because I the Lord your God am holy" (Lev 19:2; I Pet I:16). The holiness of the individual and the holiness of the people with whom that individual is joined in *koinōnia* through baptism are the fruit of the life, death, and resurrection of Jesus which is the substance of the Christian preaching. Very often one conceives the proclamation of the word as changing the world. That role may be true; but unless we see the change in terms of holiness, we have not understood how the world must ultimately reflect the image and likeness of God.

The last part of the demand and the promise that follow the first sermon in the Book of Acts is this: "You shall receive the gift of the Holy Spirit." The Spirit is the final step in the work of Jesus; indeed the Spirit is the final agent in the work of God (p. 107 above). The ultimate actions that crown Jesus' ministry include not only crucifixion and resurrection, but also the giving of the Spirit. If the proclamation of the word is the continuity of his work, it must be related to the gift of the

Spirit. A preacher like Stephen is described as "full of the Spirit" (Acts 7:54); but it is never suggested that the preacher gives the Spirit. The gift of the Spirit is from God; the preacher opens the hearts of his hearers to receive the divine gift. That may be an important observation at a time when we are very concerned about the effectiveness of the Christian message. No doubt the skills of the preacher are important; yet we must be wary of Madison Avenue's standards of promoting effectiveness, embodied for many in the nattily-dressed TV preacher, with carefully styled hair, clutching his King James Bible amid banks of flowers and a background of blond gospel singers. The ultimate effectiveness of the message is in the hands of God whose gift of the Spirit often surprises in the direction it takes—"The Spirit/wind blows where it wills" (John 3:8).

*   *   *

In concluding, I am sure that, based on a study of Acts, many other observations might be made about doctrinal priorities, but the ones I have made are in my judgment important both in Acts and for modern thought. Let me list them:

- a firm grasp of the time-conditioned character of the biblical accounts;
- an understanding that the word (*dabar*) of God is larger than preaching or the spoken word;
- the tolerability and even necessity of somewhat diverse positions so that the fullness of the divine subject may be mirrored;
- the need to adapt the message to different audiences so that it may be a meaningful word;
- the priority, necessity, and corrective value of the story of Israel without which Christ is easily misunderstood;
- the centrality of what God has done *in Christ* if a message is to be distinctively Christian;
- the different respective roles of resurrection, crucifixion, and ministry of Jesus in understanding the whole Christ—it was a crucified one who was raised, and he was crucified because he had offered the kingdom to those who by human standards were to be rejected;
- the fundamental reaction is *metanoia*, "change of mind," a task no less difficult for religious people today than it was in the time of Jesus;

■ that reaction must lead the hearers into a relation with the church and
its sacraments;
■ the goal is to bring about holiness through the forgiveness of sins and
God's somewhat unpredictable gift of the Spirit.

In reflecting on the list, one cannot help being astonished by the
profundity of the message communicated and the reactions demanded in
the early sermons narrated in Acts. If the author was partially historical
and the sermons reflected not only the 80s but something of the 30s and
40s, the first preachers accomplished a great task that teaches us much
about doctrinal priorities. They did not preach the kingdom simply as
Jesus preached it; they kept the message alive by ingeniously translating
it into another idiom. They preached the kingdom by preaching Christ
as they saw him with the perceptivity of increased faith.

That deduction supplies the observation with which I shall close the
main part of this book[137] devoted to the relation between the Bible (critically interpreted) and church doctrine. One is not faithful in communicating the biblical message (the detection of which involves critical
exegesis) unless one rethinks it in terms of meaningful contemporary issues (a rethinking in which church doctrine is formulated). The slogans,
"Preach only what is in the Bible," and "Teach only what the church
teaches," are both simplistic if they ignore the need for translating what
has been received into a new idiom to keep it alive. In this book I have
criticized liberals who in a desire to be relevant play too loose with the
tradition (including the Bible) and do not *transmit what has been received*. I have also criticized ultraconservatives who so freeze the tradition in the categories of the past they do not *translate meaningfully*
what has been received. We can be grateful that, according to the evidence of Acts, the first preachers were not people who simply transmitted what Jesus taught; they thought about what he meant and translated
it. But they did this in such a manner that it remained *his* gospel.

---

[137]As indicated in the Preface, the last two chapters are by way of appendixes and are
not part of the main theme.

Chapter 9
APPENDED NOTES ON
THE SHROUD OF TURIN

The literature on the Shroud continues to be abundant,[138] much of it provoked by the publishing of the STURP (Shroud of Turin Research Project) experiments done on October 8–13, 1978 with modern scientific instruments in a Turin palace. The reports in high technological detail have greatly enlightened the discussion of the Shroud and ruled out many possibilities. I shall not attempt to produce their results or to tell the history of the Shroud; I wish merely to insist on some clarifications that seem to be useful even after the most recent writing. I shall do this under several headings.

HOW? BY WHOM? OF WHOM?
WHY? WHERE? WHEN?

How? The recent investigations make it clear that the body-image on the Shroud is not composed of paint or liquid stain or coloring. It was not made by heating or by scorching or by radiation emanating from an engraving, a bas-relief, or a statue. It was somehow formed from a dead human body. The straw-yellow color of the body-image, which involves the oxidation and loss of water in the tops of the fibrils that formed the

---

[138]In particular, I found thought-provoking: F. C. Tribbe, *Portrait of Jesus?* (New York: Stein and Day, 1983); G. Ghiberti, *La Sepoltura di Gesù. I Vangeli e la Sindone* (Rome: P. Marietti, 1982); R. A. Wild, "The Shroud of Turin—Probably the Work of a 14th-Century Artist or Forger," *BAR* 10 (March/April 1984) 30–43.

image, would be compatible with intense radiation on or from a human body, even if the specific type of the radiant energy is not totally definable. (The latest suggestion is a lightning bolt.) The proper conclusion would seem to be that the image was produced either supernaturally or by natural forces not known to the scientists. A reader who has not yet come to a decision, however, will often get the impression from discussions by the scientists that they have tilted toward a supernatural explanation, explicitly or implicitly. I find such a tilt in the statement of R. Dinger quoted approvingly by Tribbe on p. 151: "We have absolutely no indication that the image was produced by the hand of man." Technically that is correct; but one might easily get the impression that the production was supernatural, granted the fact that "the hand of man" often means human involvement.

By Whom? If the production of the image was supernatural, the answer lies clearly in the direction of mediate or immediate divine intervention. If the production was by natural means not known to us, then a human being would have been involved in some way. Tribbe (p. 142) assures us that it was "not made by an artist, craftsman, or forger." I do not believe that we can assert that. Probably all that he means is that, since the image does not involve paint or sketching, it was not made by painting or by drafting or by crafting. But, if the image was produced by radiation in some natural way unknown to us, then the human being who took this image and preserved it could have been an artist, or a craftsman, or an alchemist, or simply someone who happened on the results. (For reasons I shall mention below, he may have duplicated those results in an instance other than the one he first discovered, namely, on a crucified body.) This may seem like nit-picking, but I think that it is important for us to admit that we know nothing about the identity of the person involved in the production and/or preservation of the image, even if his hand did not produce that image.

Of Whom? Scientists seem reasonably certain that the image on the Shroud came from a deceased human body bearing marks of scourging, wounds, and crucifixion compatible with the Gospel accounts of the death of Jesus of Nazareth. Because of the similarities to the Gospel accounts, G. R. Habermas[139] argues that there is only one chance in 225

---

[139]"The Shroud of Turin and Its Significance for Biblical Studies," *Journal of the Evangelical Theological Society* 24 (1981) 47–54.

billion, or more skeptically, one chance in 83 million that the man in the Shroud is not Jesus. Such a tendency to think only of accidental similarity to the Gospel accounts is fallacious. One could posit that an individual was *deliberately* scourged, wounded, and crucified in the manner in which the Gospels describe Jesus' death. Lest one have to posit a macabre imitation, it should be noted that those opposed to Christians sometimes "obliged" Christians by executing them in the manner of Jesus. P. A. Gramaglia[140] has argued that between A.D. 540 and 640 funeral wrappings from Palestine were numerous and crucifixions were used to mock Christians. Christians even crucified Jews for revenge. According to Gramaglia, a shroud of a man crucified as Christ could have come from a Palestinian context in the 600s. Thus, the alternative to the man in the Shroud being Jesus is not a chance resemblance in another corpse but someone deliberately crucified in imitation of Jesus.

Why? The reference given above to the statement of Tribbe, "not made by an artist, craftsman, or forger," illustrates the tendency (now rejected by Tribbe himself[141]) to think that if the Shroud is not the burial cloth of Jesus, it is a forgery. To my mind, if the Shroud was produced by natural causes unknown to us, the purpose of its dissemination needs still to be determined. Let us suppose that an individual stumbled upon an image of a dead person, produced by some energy unknown to us and not understood by him. He might have wished to imitate the process in respect to a dead crucified person in order to pass off the image as the burial cloth of Jesus Christ. That would be forgery in the classic sense: making or imitating fraudulently, especially with the intention to deceive. If the same sequence of actions took place, however, with the intention to honor the deceased crucified person, or with the intention to show people how the crucified Jesus might have looked, that would not be forgery but piety. Later purveyors of the image might well have had the intent of deceiving, but the original individual need not be so pejoratively esteemed. It is worth noting that two bishops of Troyes in the 1300s, when the Shroud of Turin was being exhibited for the first time in their diocese, insisted that this was not the burial garment of Jesus. Consequently, Clement VII allowed public exhibition of the Shroud only as a "representation" of Jesus' burial garment. Clearly, the intention of

---

[140]*L'uomo della Sindone non è Gesù Cristo* (Turin: Claudiana, 1978).
[141]*BAR* 10 (#4, 1984) 25.

Clement was not fraudulent even though in his judgment the Shroud did not contain the image of the true body of Jesus.

Where? Frequently, in reports of the scientific investigations, it is noted that the three-to-one herringbone pattern of the weaving in the Shroud was not known in France in the 14th century, that pollen from Palestine and the Near East is found in the Shroud, that the style of crucifixion through the wrists and of the crown of thorns as a cap was not the artistic convention of medieval Europe. All of these observations would tend to indicate that the image on the Shroud was not produced in France in the 1300s when the Shroud was first exhibited. It is a long jump from that observation to the assumption that the Shroud is the burial cloth of Jesus. The theory of Gramaglia cited above, which suggests that the Shroud might have been produced in Palestine at an earlier period, would eliminate some of the objections raised by science in terms of the cloth and of the pollen from plants of that area and from plants no longer extant today. It would also do justice to the observations of some that the man depicted in the Shroud had Semitic features and wore his hair in a style not known in medieval Europe. All in all then, likelihood favors the production of the Shroud in Palestine or in the Near East, whether or not it is the burial cloth of Jesus.

When? It has been observed that the Shroud betrays a perception of human anatomy and blood-flow not known to artists or even to doctors in the Middle Ages. To my mind such observations are completely irrelevant for dating if the Shroud was not the product of painting or sketching. If the Shroud was produced from a dead, crucified body by a natural means of radiation not known to us, it would have anatomical exactness no matter whether or not that body belonged to Jesus of Nazareth. If one opts for the Near East as the locus, however, a production earlier than the 14th century becomes much more plausible. It has been argued by F. Filas that the man imaged in the Shroud has coins on his eyes and that the coin on the right eye is a coin of Pontius Pilate. If true, that would be reconcilable if the Shroud is the burial cloth of Jesus. It could also be reconciled with production several centuries afterwards if someone took the effort to use a preserved coin of Pilate in adorning the body of a deceased crucified person. Obviously that could be for fraudulent reasons, or could be again seen as a pious touch if someone were trying to show how the burial of Jesus might have looked. R. Hachlili and A. Kilbrew[142] argue that the custom of burying people with coins on their eyes is not a first-century custom but a later Jewish custom. If the Shroud was the product of a later period, someone might have been imitating the custom of the Jews in his own time. Overall, then, one can say very little about the exact dating of the Shroud although a date in the first millennium would seem most plausible.

None of the above observations excludes the possibility that the Shroud was the burial cloth of Jesus, or that it was produced by supernatural means. The real purpose is to make certain that other possibilities are not overlooked.

ENDURING PROBLEMS OF ARTISTRY VS. NON-ARTISTRY

Granting the scientific discoveries that seem to exclude any type of painting or drawing, or even scorching from an artistic model, we must still face the difficulty that certain features in the Shroud suit artistry better than they suit reproduction of nature. Some of those problems affect the body-image; even greater problems affect the blood stains.

The Body-Image. Scientists seem to agree that the body-image was not produced by contact between the Shroud and the body enveloped in it. Nevertheless, the face and the hands of the image stand out with particular emphasis—a fact not totally explicable by the height of those parts of a reclining body, for the chest seems to have lesser delineation even though that should have been as elevated as the hands which lie over the genital area. On the other hand, in the back image, the buttocks are only faintly outlined. It has been noted that the navel of the Shroud image is either absent or almost invisible. Is this an element of modesty or of theology? It may be remembered that frequently Adam is pictured without a navel (an intelligible absence because of the biblical story of his creation), and some may have thought that such an anatomical peculiarity might befit the new Adam. Wild suggests a possible connection with the theology of the virginal birth of Jesus—not the conception, but the birth as a miracle that did not involve a violation of Mary's organs. Another problem is the attention given to the covering of the genitals. In the Shroud, the man's hands are crossed on the genital area with the right

---

[142]*Biblical Archaeologist* 46 (1983) 147–52.

hand completely covering any nudity. Wild notes that the body imaged in the Shroud is portrayed as relaxed in death, but in a relaxed position a man's joined hands will not cover his genitals if he lies on his back. Either the body has to be tilted forward and the arms stretched downward, or the elbows have to be propped up on the side and the wrists drawn together to hold the hands in place over the genital area. In the Shroud image also, the right arm is exceedingly long and the fingers of the right hand almost disproportionate, in order to allow the modest covering. Again, such a feature would be more understandable if the Shroud were an artistic production reflecting the interests of another era.

The Blood on the Shroud. The blood-images are, unlike the body-image, true stains and appear as a positive, not a negative, in a photo. They are distinct and not smeared. If one examines them closely, it becomes extremely difficult to understand how they were made in any theory of the origins of the Shroud. There seems to be no great distinction in terms of time (drying) or of preservation (smearing) in the blood produced by the scourging, by the crown of thorns, by the nail wounds, and by the wound in the side. (If I understand correctly, a certain separation of blood from serum has begun in various stains, and certainly in the wound from the side.) Obviously, no matter who the subject of the image was, the scourging would have had to take place *before* he was crucified. Moreover, the wounds on the head and the arms show a downward flow of blood, almost as if the Shroud were stained when the figure was still erect on the cross, or at least held up vertically. Yet the blood from the wound on the side and seemingly that of the feet show a sideward flow as if the body were lying prone. Once again all of this could be quite intelligible from an artist who was attempting to catch in one picture the various moments of Jesus' suffering. It is very difficult to understand in a shroud that preserves the image of Jesus' *dead* body.

Most have assumed that the blood-images on the Shroud mean that the body was not washed, no matter what the Jewish law on that issue may have been in the time of Jesus. Others have argued that the body was washed and that the wounds began to flow again after death, even though that will not settle the problem of the direction of the flow. In either case one must deal with the issue of when the Shroud enveloped the body. Did it envelop the body as it was taken from the cross? The clear distinctness of the body-image as lying flat, and the lack of smudging of the blood stains make it almost inconceivable that the crumpled body was deposited in the Shroud as it came off a cross. Almost equally inconceivable is that the cloth lay on the uneven ground and the body was deposited on top of it and then carried in this shroud to the tomb or place of burial. If one argues that some other cloth or wrappings were used to transfer the body from the cross to a flat place or slab on which the Shroud lay, and that only there was the body enveloped in the Shroud, one must then explain the clarity or non-smudging of the blood from the wounds. P. Barbet[143] tried to deal with this problem. He proposed that the body of Jesus, rigid in death as ''an iron bar'' because of tetanic contractions of the muscles, was taken down still on the cross-beam or *patibulum*. Then, horizontal and stiff as a board, it was transported to the tomb by five bearers. Two of them supported the *patibulum* to which the top part of the body was attached; two held a tightly twisted cloth under the mid-back; one held up the crossed legs by the right heel— the latter being the only flesh touched by the bearers' hands. Only in the tomb was the corpse taken off the *patibulum* and deposited on the Shroud. Some will find the cortege grotesque; others will doubt that the Roman soldiers were so obliging about lending the *patibulum*.

Those who argue that the Shroud is a supernaturally produced image of the dead body of Jesus of Nazareth must really posit two distinct miracles: the transmission of the body-image by some form of energy to the Shroud as a negative picture, and the positive reproduction of blood wounds made when he was scourged, crowned with thorns, nailed to the cross, and after his death, with all those wounds preserved almost as they were made.

These problems make Wild insist that the Shroud is still most probably the work of a 14th-century artist or forger. Those who are more receptive of the scientists' arguments that a 14th-century date is not plausible, and that the body-image is not the production of manual art, are more likely to argue that, while the body-image may have resulted from some discovery of radiant energy no longer known to us, the blood stains were in some other way the work of an artist—even though that still creates problems with the scientists' conclusions. Perhaps the most perplexing sentence in Tribbe's book is on p. 146 and is italicized so that it might catch our notice: *''The blood-images were present on the cloth before the body-images were 'placed or developed' on it.''* This sug-

---

[143]*A Doctor at Calvary* (New York: Kenedy, 1953) 129–32, 136–37.

gestion from the researcher's report is a great difficulty for many theories of how the Shroud was produced.

THE SHROUD AND THE EVANGELISTS

Those who are favorable to the thesis that the Shroud is an image of the dead body of Jesus have insisted that it is remarkably concordant with the information provided by the four Gospels. In fact, some of them have been quite critical of biblical scholars who do not find the Gospel accounts concordant, almost as if the Shroud disproves modern biblical criticism and shows the scholars to be skeptical rationalists.[144] Certainly the Shroud appears to presuppose material from the four Gospels, for only the Synoptics mention a single enveloping burial linen, the *sindōn*, while only John mentions the wound in the side. The sharp disagreement among the Gospels, whereby in John a more-than-ample amount of spices is provided before the burial of Jesus, in Matthew spices are not mentioned at all, and in Mark and Luke the women prepare to bring spices only after the burial, is harmonized by various Shroud enthusiasts into two anointings of the body, even though that runs against the clear understanding of the evangelists. Some biblical scholars, such as A. Feuillet and J. A. T. Robinson, have attempted in detail to show that the biblical accounts are not irreconcilable with the details of the Shroud. For instance, the *othonia* ("cloth wrappings") of John are sometimes assumed to be a collective which could possibly be the same as the *sindōn*; or the *soudarion* ("piece of cloth") of John is either identified with the *sindōn* or interpreted as a chin band which some find depicted in the Shroud. Be all of that as it may or may not, J. A. T. Robinson has a point when he says that only with great difficulty from a reading of the Gospels would one imagine the burial cloth of Jesus to be in the form in which the Shroud is preserved. The lengthwise image of front and back, so that the Shroud is folded over the head rather than folded sidewise, is rather startling granted the Gospel descriptions.

Two observations may be useful without entering this very complicated area. In his excellently balanced book, Ghiberti makes a point

---

[144]On this point this appended chapter comes together with the main theme of the book and illustrates another attempt to dismiss historical biblical criticism because of preconceptions.

that a true biblical critic cannot assume that any of the Gospels necessarily give us exact details about the burial of Jesus. Each evangelist may be describing that burial (which took place decades before the Gospels were written) in terms of the Jewish customs he knows in his time and in his area. Therefore, lack of agreement between the Shroud and the biblical accounts is really not a major feature if one argues that the Shroud is the historical burial garment, even though most Shroud enthusiasts seem to think that agreement with the Gospels is a matter of life or death. More important is the issue raised by Robinson which may be used in an inverse way. If the Shroud were known to any of the evangelists, would he have described the burial in the way he did? Certainly the Synoptics should have described a wound in the side of Christ, and John should have been more clear about the nature of the burial cloth. But above all, any evangelist who knew the Shroud should have mentioned the marvelous preservation of the image of Jesus. Silence on this subject is particularly startling in the Fourth Gospel which makes a point of describing the burial clothes left by Jesus in the tomb. (I for one do not find convincing that a conspiracy of silence existed among the early Christians lest they give offense to the Jews about having a human image of the Saviour in their midst.) In the early argumentation about the resurrection, the Shroud would have been a marvelous apologetic proof over against the Jews; but no mention of it is found in the Gospels, nor even a description that betrays knowledge of it. This argumentation does not disprove the Shroud but should make us aware that the history of its preservation is more mysterious than one could guess from discussions of where it was before exhibition in France in the 14th century.

Discussions of the Shroud, I find (somewhat like discussions of the virginal conception of Jesus), seem to arouse passions and polemic almost as if the consideration of questions is a challenge to faith. These questions have been presented as irenically as possible by one who has no set opinion about the Shroud but wishes to be certain that difficulties are not overlooked. The scientific facts were reported to the best of a non-scientist's understanding and not to favor any particular theory. [145]

---

[145] A scientist informs me that the disproportionate length of arm and hand (p. 152 above) may be related to other distortions in the Shroud, e.g., the front of the image is longer than the back. Logically, the blood images could have been produced before the body image if the former came about at burial and the latter at resurrection.

Chapter 10
APPENDED NOTES ON R. LAURENTIN'S EXEGESIS OF THE INFANCY NARRATIVES

I n Chapter 4 I discussed R. Laurentin's recent book on the infancy narratives (see footnote 67) from the aspect of his misunderstanding and even misrepresenting the work of historical-critical exegetes—a treatment matching the theme of that chapter. I passed no comments there on the quality of Laurentin's own exegetical statements about the meaning of these narratives. But since his book has been the subject of intensive propaganda in the ultraconservative press, it might be useful for me to reprint substantially the section of my article in *Marianum* where I critiqued that exegesis.

Laurentin devotes a third of his volume to semiotic or structuralist exegesis. Leaving aside such questions as authorship, dating, and origin, the semiotic study of the Scriptures, popular largely in French circles, concentrates on the internal structure of a text as a guide to its meaning. While some find this approach excessively mathematical in counting words and grammatical patterns, or excessively artificial in detecting structures to which the author may never have alluded, in principle it can contribute some useful insights to the larger picture of exegesis, *if it complements other forms of exegesis* (see p. 20 above). One should beware, however, of exaggerated claims suggesting that this semiotic/structuralist exegesis will revolutionize our understanding of the infancy narratives. Above all, it is irresponsible to propose that semiotics can help establish the historicity of the infancy narratives, since *ex professo* this approach does not deal with historical issues. As a caution about the overall contribution of semiotics to the infancy narratives, let me quote from the able French scholar L. Monloubou who reviewed Laurentin's book in *Esprit et Vie* (93 [Nov. 24, 1983] 648). He asks pointblank whether Laurentin's semiotic approach really does something new for the interpretation of the infancy narratives, and here I translate his response:

> Our author [Laurentin] thinks so. I do not. According to my perception, this surging ocean of semiotics whose foaming waves swept over the tranquil beaches of exegesis is now in the process of retreating. It has left certain places on the exegetical beach reshaped; it also leaves various debris. An improper amount of importance given to the formal elements of a text irresistibly recalls the excesses of formal logic so appreciated by a decadent scholasticism.

Be that as it may, I shall concentrate on the non-semiotic sections of Laurentin's work. I begin with some general remarks. Despite the length of the volume (633 pp.), in my judgment it is not a comprehensive commentary. For instance, although Laurentin devotes 293 pp. to textual, literary, and semiotic exegesis of Luke, he devotes only 56 pp. to the exegesis of Matthew. Why this unbalanced 6-to-1 favoritism toward Luke? The key, I suggest, lies in the fact that Mary plays a relatively small part in Matthew's infancy narrative and the large part in Luke's. Laurentin is really giving us a mariological study of the infancy narratives, and in his efforts all texts are not treated equally. That suggestion may also explain why Laurentin treats Luke before Matthew.

While there are many points I would agree with, I wish now to present some items that I found quite defective in Laurentin's more traditional sections of exegesis. In each instance, after the page number from his *Evangiles,* I will present almost telegraphically Laurentin's view; then I shall add my own comment.

P. 7 (also p. 385). One argument in favor of the historicity of the infancy narratives is that, if the evangelists were giving a theological construction of Jesus' origins, their obvious solution would have been that Jesus came down from heaven. *Comment:* I find nothing obvious about the second solution; it would scarcely have occurred to *Jews* who came to believe in Christ, for there is no Jewish expectation of a human figure coming down from heaven (unless one thinks of Elijah returning). Supporting the thesis that Jesus came down from heaven, Laurentin finds a whole series of NT texts. I would be much more conservative (John, possibly some Pauline hymns, Hebrews), for very few NT authors indicate explicitly a heavenly pre-existence.

P. 7 (also p. 385). There was a firm local tradition at Nazareth that Jesus was not the son of Joseph; and the Gospels constantly avoid calling Jesus the son of Joseph except through the lips of his adversaries [including John 1:45!] or in contexts where the language of daily life is clearly "rectified." *Comment:* What Laurentin's remark disguises is that *only once* (Mark 6:3) is Jesus called the son of the other parent, Mary, while five times he is called the son of Joseph or of the carpenter. There is not the slightest evidence that anyone at Nazareth thought of Jesus as not being the son of Joseph—the one Marcan passage may have mentioned Mary simply because Joseph was dead.

P. 30. For translating *kecharitomenē* (Luke 1:28), Laurentin cites Chrysostom who knew his Greek language well. *Comment:* Laurentin should have asked himself whether the Chrysostom interpretation was more influenced by the mariology of Chrysostom's time than by his knowledge of the language.

P. 54. Galatians 4:4, "born of a woman," refers to the virginal conception because otherwise Paul would have used the natural expression "born of man." *Comment:* Has Laurentin any evidence of "born of man" as a commonly-used idiom? As stressed in *MNT* (pp. 42–43), "born of woman" is a common Jewish idiom applicable to every human being—all are born of woman (see p. 88 above).

P. 101. He mentions two lines of interpretation of the sword's piercing Mary's own soul: One in which it pierces the daughter of Zion (Mary as Israel), and one that involves the suffering of Christ himself. *Comment:* He should have discussed the likelihood that the text simply concerns Mary herself as described in Luke's subsequent Gospel narrative.

P. 102. Luke does not mention Mary as present at the cross, even as he does not mention her presence at the birth of John the Baptist, even though he intends to signify in both cases that she was there "It is in the style of Luke." *Comment:* I would judge rather that "It is in the style of Laurentin" to make such an unprovable affirmation. How can one seriously argue from complete silence that Mary is at the cross in Luke's Gospel?

P. 110. Part of the reason his parents did not understand Jesus in

2:49–50 when he said, "Did you not know that I must be in my Father's House?", is because he was speaking of his return to his Father in death. *Comment:* This highly speculative exegesis would have Luke expecting the reader to connect the Temple scene and the crucifixion because both occurred at Passover. Moreover, since Laurentin assumes historicity, he is dependent on an unprovable assumption about Jesus' knowledge of the future.

P. 189. "I do not know man" in Luke's annunciation is like "I do not smoke"—determination is expressed. *Comment:* Laurentin offers no adequate discussion of the terminology of objections raised in OT annunciations. Are they, too, expressions of determination, or simply descriptions of the state of the speaker (Gen 18:12; Exod 3:11; Judg 6:15; also Luke 1:18)?

P. 379 (also p. 439). The marvelous in Matthew's infancy narrative is on a very discreet level [!]. Many features in it "recoup" historical fact; for there were astrologers in the Orient, and Qumran had a horoscope of the Messiah, and Herod was a cruel king. *Comment:* Laurentin does not alert the reader sufficiently to the fact that verisimilitude does not establish historicity. If one *were* writing historical fiction, the cruel king and the astrologers would make the story plausible, not necessarily historical.

P. 379. An argument for the historicity of Matthew's infancy narrative is that the events do not fit well the five Scripture citations. If the events were fictional, the author would have made them match the citations. *Comment:* All this proves is that Matthew himself did not create the events of his narrative. If they came to him from an earlier account, there would remain an awkwardness between the events and the citations Matthew added. The real issue is whether the earlier account was historical (and one cannot simply *assume* that Matthew was in a position to know whether what he used was historical).

Pp. 383–84. Those who have found insurmountable contradictions between Matthew 1–2 and Luke 1–2 have succeeded only in distorting the texts from their sense. The time of the coming of the magi need not be settled, nor its relationship to Luke 2 where the parents return peaceably through Jerusalem to Nazareth. This is a *concordia discordantium*. *Comment:* Oratory cannot disguise a failure to deal with major problems. One can allow the full and undistorted sense of each Gospel text and still find that two texts disagree.

P. 386. John 1:13 proves the virginal conception. *Comment:* Laurentin owes his reader an acknowledgment that this interpretation of the verse is a minority view based on no existing Greek text. Why does he not treat the arguments on both sides of the issue?

P. 386. Luke 1:32 referred to the pre-existence of Jesus because Son of God is mentioned before Son of David. *Comment:* The relative importance of the two ideas may have governed the order of precedence, and there is no evidence elsewhere in Luke of pre-existence christology.

P. 391. We have a measure of how Luke favors historicity over fiction in the fact that he includes in the infancy narrative no healing and no multiplication of the loaves, as a fictional writer might have done in anticipating the ministry. *Comment:* Fiction can be shaped in many ways, and so the argument is illogical (even though I do not think the narrative is fiction).

P. 411. Matthew knew well that he had omitted kings' names in his genealogy. *Comment:* Proof?

P. 414. After rebuking scholars who cannot reconcile the two genealogies (these scholars will pass away and the genealogies will remain), Laurentin (p. 417) reconciles the genealogies by positing various adoptions. *Comment:* Proof for these adoptions? Possibility does not establish fact.

P. 421. Matthew avoids all idea of *hieros (theios) gamos* (a sexual union between a divine male and a human female) in the conception of Jesus because for Matthew "spirit" is feminine in the maternal Semitic language. *Comment:* Does Laurentin's Matthew expect the *Greek* readers of his Gospel to know this? The reasoning is weak even though the affirmation about *hieros gamos* is correct.

P. 429. Paul knew about the infancy of Jesus but "he was not without conceptual embarrassment" about the matter. (See also pp. 53, 387.) *Comment:* The figure of the easily embarrassed Paul is a newcomer on the stage of biblical exegesis.

P. 446. Laurentin criticizes the view that the *Magnificat* might refer to more than Israel (universalist interpretation). *Comment:* He fails to distinguish between what the canticle originally meant and how Luke uses it—a distinction I carefully made (*Birth,* p. 365).

P. 449. If the *Magnificat* was transmitted, *without doubt* Mary herself took it up and actualized it in the primitive Christian community of Jerusalem. *Comment:* "Without doubt" hides a "without proof." To

Laurentin's credit is his recognition on p. 450 that he does not pretend to furnish proof for the hypothesis that Mary memorized the *Benedictus* and passed it on because Zechariah had died. A similar hypothesis is offered for the *Nunc dimittis* on p. 451.

P. 460. An argument for the historicity and traditional character of the Lucan infancy narrative is that Luke could not "create a text of this profoundness and unheard of coherence." *Comment:* Such a subjective judgment about the quality of a narrative has little value in establishing historicity. If Luke did not originally compose (note my avoidance of the loaded term "create") this narrative, then someone else composed it. How do we know that that person could control the historicity of the incidents therein recounted?

P. 460. Laurentin argues for historicity thus: "If Matthew and Luke searched for what could have been the revelation of God about the origin of Christ, why would they have found *nothing?* And if they really found nothing, why would they have had recourse to fiction?" *Comment:* There is an intermediary between finding nothing in the tradition and finding completely historical narratives, namely, finding that according to the tradition, Jesus was conceived of Mary by the Holy Spirit. See above (p. 82) for my comments about the false dichotomy involved in seeing only the alternatives of invented fiction and historical narratives.

P. 461. Complaining how biblical critics see religion as subjectivity and most events in the infancy narratives as fiction, Laurentin finds even Cardinal Daniélou defective because he did not think that the *Gloria* of the angels (Luke 2) was heard by the shepherds, but thought it might come from the Christian liturgy. Such skepticism can be refuted by the proved experiences of Catherine Labouré and Bernadette. *Comment:* None.

P. 464. Laurentin classifies my theory about the star of Matthew in terms of a theologoumenon which takes up the prophecy of Balaam about the star of David. *Comment:* The Balaam passage may supply the coloring of the Matthean account; I think it likely that the basic idea came from a *retrospective* attempt to connect a celestial phenomenon with the birth of Jesus. The Balaam story may have helped to specify the phenomenon as a star.

Clearly I do not think that many aspects of Laurentin's exegesis are helpful; but with the French book translated into English, readers can judge for themselves the profundity of the work.

LIST OF ABBREVIATIONS

AR   *Antioch and Rome* by R. E. Brown and J. P. Meier (New York: Paulist, 1983)

BAR   *Biblical Archaeology Review*

BM   *The Birth of the Messiah* by R. E. Brown (Garden City, NY: Doubleday, 1977)

BRCFC   *Biblical Reflections on Crises Facing the Church* by R. E. Brown (New York: Paulist, 1975)

BTB   *Biblical Theology Bulletin*

CBQ   *Catholic Biblical Quarterly*

CMB   *The Critical Meaning of the Bible* by R. E. Brown (New York: Paulist, 1981)

DBS   *Enchiridion Symbolorum,* ed. by H. Denzinger, C. Bann-wart, and A. Schönmetzer (32nd ed.; Freiburg: Herder, 1963)

DVII   *The Documents of Vatican II,* ed. by W. M. Abbott and J. Gallagher (New York: Guild, 1966)

JBC   *The Jerome Biblical Commentary,* ed. by R. E. Brown, J. A. Fitzmyer, and R. E. Murphy (Englewood Cliffs, NJ: Prentice-Hall, 1968)

MNT   *Mary in the New Testament,* ed. by R. E. Brown, K. P. Donfried, *et al.* (Philadelphia: Fortress; New York: Paulist, 1978)

NT   New Testament

NTS   *New Testament Studies*

OCTBI   *Official Catholic Teachings: Bible Interpretation,* ed. by J. J. Megivern (Consortium Book; Wilmington, NC: McGrath, 1978)

OT   Old Testament

PB   *Priest and Bishop: Biblical Reflections* by R. E. Brown (New York: Paulist, 1970)

PCTSA   *Proceedings of the Catholic Theological Society of America*

RSS   *Rome and the Study of Scripture* (7th ed.; St. Meinrad, IN: Grail, 1962)

TBT   *The Bible Today*

VCBRJ   *The Virginal Conception and Bodily Resurrection of Jesus* by R. E. Brown (New York: Paulist, 1973)

ACKNOWLEDGMENTS

Along with much never previously published material, sections from the following earlier pieces I had written were reused in whole or in part, often with heavy adaptation, in this book:

"New Testament Background for the Concept of Local Church," *PCTSA* 36 (1981) 1–14, contributed to Chapter 7.

"Mary in the New Testament and in Catholic Life," *America* 146 (#19; May 15, 1982) 374–79, contributed to Chapter 5.

"Not Jewish Christianity and Gentile Christianity but Types of Jewish/Gentile Christianity," *CBQ* 45 (1983) 74–79, contributed to Chapter 7.

"Diverse Views of the Spirit in the New Testament," *Worship* 57 (#3, May 1983) 225–36, contributed to Chapter 6.

"Preaching in the Acts of the Apostles," in *A New Look at Preaching,* ed. J. Burke (Good News Studies 7; Wilmington: Glazier, 1983) 59–73, contributed to Chapter 8.

"Brief Observations on the Shroud of Turin," *BTB* 14 (Oct. 1984) 145–48, contributed to Chapter 9.

"Liberals, Ultraconservatives, and the Misinterpretation of Catholic Biblical Exegesis," *Cross Currents* 34 (#3, Fall 1984) 311–28, contributed to Chapters 3 and 4.

"More Polemical than Instructive: R. Laurentin on the Infancy Narratives," *Marianum* 47 (1985) 15–38 (an article, which along with the next contribution, represents an adapted written form of the T. V. Moore Lecture given at the Catholic University [Wash. DC] on Sept. 29, 1984), contributed to Chapters 4 and 10.

"Historical Critical Exegesis and Attempts at Revisionism," *TBT* 23 (#3, May 1985) 157-65, contributed to Chapter 1.

INDEX

BOOKS BY RAYMOND E. BROWN (1986)

Paulist Press
New Testament Essays
Priest and Bishop
The Virginal Conception and Bodily Resurrection of Jesus
Peter in the New Testament (editor)
Biblical Reflections on Crises Facing the Church
Mary in the New Testament (editor)
The Community of the Beloved Disciple
The Critical Meaning of the Bible
Antioch and Rome (with J. P. Meier)
The Churches the Apostles Left Behind
Biblical Exegesis and Church Doctrine

Doubleday
The Gospel According to John (2 vols., Anchor Bible Commentary)
The Birth of the Messiah
The Epistles of John (Anchor Bible Commentary)

Liturgical Press (Collegeville, Minn.)
The Gospel and Epistles of John (3rd ed.; NT Reading Guide 13)
The Book of Deuteronomy (OT Reading Guide)
An Adult Christ at Christmas
A Crucified Christ in Holy Week

Prentice Hall
The Jerome Biblical Commentary (editor)

Macmillan
Jesus God and Man

Michael Glazier (Wilmington, Del)
Recent Discoveries and the Biblical World

*Many of the above have been published in England by
Geoffrey Chapman*